No One Knows When It's a Good Day

And a few other things I have said on Sunday Mornings

*To Pat —
One of God's good
gifts —
Tom Starnes*

Thomas Starnes

authorHOUSE®

AuthorHouse™ LLC
1663 Liberty Drive
Bloomington, IN 47403
www.authorhouse.com
Phone: 1-800-839-8640

© 2014 Thomas Starnes. All rights reserved.

No part of this book may be reproduced, stored in a retrieval system, or
transmitted by any means without the written permission of the author.

NRSV
Scripture quotations marked NRSV are taken from the New Revised Standard
Version of the Bible, Copyright © 1989, by the Division of Christian
Education of the National Council of the Churches of Christ in the United
States of America. Used by permission. All rights reserved. Website

Published by AuthorHouse   09/25/2014

ISBN: 978-1-4969-4193-0 (sc)
ISBN: 978-1-4969-4192-3 (e)

Library of Congress Control Number: 2014917216

Any people depicted in stock imagery provided by Thinkstock are models,
and such images are being used for illustrative purposes only.
Certain stock imagery © Thinkstock.

This book is printed on acid-free paper.

Because of the dynamic nature of the Internet, any web addresses or links contained in
this book may have changed since publication and may no longer be valid. The views
expressed in this work are solely those of the author and do not necessarily reflect the
views of the publisher, and the publisher hereby disclaims any responsibility for them.

Contents

Introduction ix

1. No One Knows When it's a Good Day..........................1
2. One of God's Favorite Words 6
3. Teach Us To Pray 12
4. Stopping Short 18
5. I Never Promised You a Rose Garden..........................22
6. The Courage of One's Doubts 27
7. The Nativity's Naiveté 31
8. A Very Present Help 37
9. Riding Out the Storm 41
10. Slender Threads 45
11. Living between the Times..51
12. Believing Without Seeing 56
13. God's Foolishness is Our Wisdom 62
14. Philip and the Ethiopian Eunuch 67
15. Handling Life's Second Bests 72
16. Made for More than This 77
17. The Faith of Job 81
18. All I Have Needed 86
19. Faith Alters Appearances...91
20. God's Neighborliness 97
21. Is the Lord Among Us 102
22. The Hound of Heaven 107
23. Life's Ups and Downs...111
24. Soul Struggles 116
25. What a Heaven's For..120
26. Is it True 126

This, my first, and last, book of sermons is lovingly
dedicated to that covenant community known as
the Hickory Hill United Methodist Church,
In Dagsboro, Delaware,
who welcomed me, called me "pastor," and made me feel,
that even though I was approaching the four score marker in my life,
I still had something worthwhile to say.

INTRODUCTION

When I wrote my spiritual memoir, Through Fear to Faith, my daughter insisted that I include a chapter on preaching, her stated reason being that preaching had been such a vital part of my faith journey that I had to have something to say on the subject in any book I might write about my faith. So I did have something to say about preaching in the book, and in the process mentioned a few sermons – just little snippets from them. Well, some who read the book expressed an interest in reading more than just those "little snippets," and some, even, went so far as to suggest that I toss them in with some other sermons and make them into a book.

It was not an appealing suggestion for me. Sermon books by minor league preachers do not fly off the shelves. Sermons are more than words on a page. Philips Brooks of long ago preaqching fame listed personality as a vital part in any effective sermon. So it's hard for a sermon to make it as a stand-alone thing; it needs to be accompanied by a preacher, a congregation and a worshipful setting. None of which can be found in a book.

But over the years since, my mind has changed. No, I still believe that most folks – even church-going folks – aren't clamoring to get their hands on some preacher's words. So why did I decide to go public with some of what I have said over the past fifty-five or so years?

My mind started warming up to the idea of putting together a book of sermons as I sat in the garage going through the process of tossing into the recycling bin a lifetime of sermon manuscripts – hardly seems an apt word to tack on to those yellow legal pad handwritten sheets. We had paid movers over the years to lug these boxes from place to place because my son Tommy had told me never to throw any of them away. But as the years rolled on, and I had witnessed surviving family members having to deal with left over "stuff," I decided that the time had come for me to assist my children and start shedding some household pounds.

Early on in that process of dumping, though, it occurred to me that those yellow sheets deserved some respect – a decent burial, you could say. No, there was no reason to keep them all. But maybe I could pick out a few that had meant something to me, and hopefully to some others who had sat out in those pews in front of me down through the years. It seemed a bit unseemly (a good preacher word) just to toss all that blood, sweat and tears into an oversized garbage can with a bunch of newspapers and empty cereal boxes.

So I have tied a few of them up in a gift box of sorts. I will treasure this precious memory of the part of this preaching life that I so enjoyed. It could also be that my children, though they had to sit through some of them, might look to it as a reminder of the faith of their father. And even though my millennial grandchildren already do not spend a lot of time with books, some day they, too, might pick it up and catch a glimpse, at least, of their Pop Pop's faith.

On most Sundays when I stood to preach, the first words out of my mouth were, "May the words of my mouth and the meditations of our hearts, be acceptable in thy sight, O Lord, our strength and our Redeemer." I pray that same prayer as I send these sermons on their way. Trusting, as I always did, that "the wind blows where it will," and, to mix metaphors, some seed just might fall on receptive soil.

No One Knows When it's a Good Day

Exactly when the smiley yellow faces began popping up ordering me to have a nice day I am not at all sure. It occurs to me, though, that it was in the early seventies when people – all kinds of people: store clerks, bank tellers, friends even – joined forces with the smiley yellow faces telling me to "have a nice day," or its counterpart, "have a good day." Some even began issuing their own revised version: "Have a good one."

At first, they were a pleasant few words to hear; something rather nice about being told to have a good day. Familiarity may, in some instances, breed contempt. It may also spawn suspicion, as it did for me, after being told repeatedly on multiple days to "have a good one," I began to question the sincerity of the comment.

One morning when the woman behind the counter handed me my change and issued her command to me about the quality of day I should have, my mind did not head to an examination of her motives: did she really mean what she said, or was this simply a replacement for "so long" or "see you" on her list of expressions used to send you on your way. Truth is, my thoughts were not about her at all, they were about the command she had just given me: "Have a good day."

For starters I wondered whether the choice was up to me – the choice about the nature of my day. Could I choose to have a good day? Was it really that simple? Could I get up each morning and command my day to be good? Am I in charge of quality control when it comes to fashioning my days, I asked myself? And it occurred to me that maybe – just maybe – I wasn't seated at the switch in command central pushing the buttons that might make my day a good one.

Simply because a lot of life is handed to us, isn't it – like that beautifully warm day at the beach early one August. Our family and my wife's brother's family had taken over my sister's beach house for a week of splashing in the ocean, building sand castles and fishing. Wave's brother loved to fish.

Which is what he and I and our two oldest sons were doing when a coast guard officer pulled up alongside our rented boat with a message that we should come ashore immediately, where we were told that my wife's father's heart had, quite unexpectedly, given out, standing our planned for good day on its head.

Chance occurrences, interruptions, sudden changes, are some of life's givens. Samuel Taylor Coleridge never completed his poem, Kubla Khan. In a drug induced sleep one afternoon, his mind was bombarded with images and expressions that would have required two to three hundred lines of verse – lines that he remembered when he awoke and began to write. Then came a knock at the door – an interruption by a "person on business from Porlock"—and Coleridge was never able to capture more than some eight or ten scattered lines and images.

"Stuff happens" has become conventional wisdom, and some potentially good days have become actually bad days. No one planned it that way. It just happened. If the people involved could have commanded their day to be good, they most certainly would have done that. And maybe they did, but their man from Porlock came knocking and altered the course of that day.

It is this capriciousness factor of life that seems to be missing in many of the "take charge of your life" books, making William Dyer's "Pulling Your Own Strings" seem just as superficial as William Henley's "I am the master of my fate, the captain of my soul." We can do worse than having a therapist – maybe even a life coach – on retainer to assist us in making the most of the three score and ten – more or less – that we have been given.

But I have sat with too many people whose days were being clouded over by circumstances out of their control. If only they could command the clouds to roll away – the ones that were blocking the sun on this particular day – how swiftly they would move to do that, but they couldn't. Those clouds had minds of their own.

So, the next time someone says to me, "Have a good day," perhaps I will ask them for suggestions as to how I might bring that off.

Another thought I had after the woman told me to have a good day was this: if I could order up a good day what would it be like? Would there be no sadness on my good day – no pain or discomfort of any kind? Yogi Berra was asked what he liked about school, and he answered, "Recess." If we could tailor make our days, would we choose to leave out all the bad and all the stressors?

Let's say we could go about fashioning ourselves a good day, and after determining that there would be no unpleasantness in any good day of ours, how do we know if something is really good or really bad? "No one knows when it's a good day" says the Hindu proverb. Is that true?

There is a Biblical basis for at least giving it a second thought. Most of us know the story of Joseph, Jacob's favored son. His older brothers sell him into slavery; bring his animal blood soaked "cloak of many colors" back to their father, convincing him that this preferred child of his is dead. Joseph, however, living in Pharaoh's house, rises in the chain of command and, in a position of power, is able to take care of his family through some pretty lean years. Eventually, Joseph makes himself known to his brothers, Jacob dies, and the brothers fret that since the father is not around anymore it will be payback time for Joseph: he will exact his revenge.

So the brothers concoct a story about a death bed plea by their father that Joseph will forgive his brothers, and Joseph listens to their trumped up account, and then says:

> "Do not be afraid! Am I in the place of God? Even though you meant it for evil, God meant it for good."

How do you know what it is that's good about a day, or, for that matter, what is bad? Lin Yutang tells a story about an old man who lived with his son in an abandoned fort. One night the old man's only horse wanders off, and when his neighbors gather to comfort him in his time of ill fortune, the old man says, "How do you know this is ill fortune?" A week later, the horse returns bringing with him a herd of wild horses, and the neighbors come calling to celebrate this bit of good fortune, only to have the old man repeat his question, changing just one word, "How do you know this is good fortune?" Days later the old man's son is thrown from one of the horses, suffering a broken leg and the neighbors come calling to celebrate this bit of ill fortune. The old man asks his question again, changing the one word. In less than a week a military draft is ordered and the old man's son, because of the broken leg, does not go marching off to war, and when the neighbors call to give thanks for this good fortune, the old man again sends them home with his question challenging their assessment of the situation.

There is truth to the Hindu proverb, isn't there? Haven't some of our supposed bad days turned out to be good days? That awful day almost a half century ago, when severe anxiety put me in such a state of panic that I feared for my sanity, seemed anything but good. It was the day, however, that forced me to find a therapist and begin to peel away phobic layers that I had used for years to keep a lid on my fears.

This notion that we can't really know whether a day is good or bad is not just Hindu wisdom. It's rooted in my faith tradition. Throughout those early days of wilderness wanderings, on any given day they wondered as they wandered. And as the bad days piled up – far outnumbering, in their minds, at least, the good days – it occurred to them that God had sent them on some sort of snipe hunt. It was only as they looked back on some of those long, hard, slogs, that they detected the hand of God and began to look upon some of those worst of times as the best of times.

So to all of you who hope I "have a good one," please know that although I appreciate your well wishes, let me suggest that the next time you send me on my way, try saying something like this:

Tom, I hope this day proves good for you; that whatever happens – whatever you experience – will be used by God to serve some useful purpose in your life, and further, that because of this day – with whatever it brings – your life will be richer and fuller, and you will have grown.

Since most of us don't have time to say all that in passing, and no doubt that, too, would get stale from overexposure, just say to me, "May God go with you." Living every day with a consciousness of God's presence has to be a good day, regardless.

One of God's Favorite Words

When preaching from the lectionary dribbled its way into the lives of some of us more liturgically minded Methodists – those of us who wanted to lay claim to our Anglican Church roots – it took some of the angst out of my sermon preparation. Gone were those Monday morning sweats that accompanied either my looking for a topic or a scripture verse to make the case for the topic I had already selected. Having three lessons and a psalm served up each week at least narrowed the focus.

It did not, however, take away all the pain of sermon writing. Especially on those weeks when I could not, for the life of me, see why the lectionary compilers strung that collection of verses together. Even though I knew – having been told by seasoned lectionary preachers – that there would not always be a unifying thread weaving its way through the lessons, my puzzle loving mind just couldn't let that bit of homiletical conventional wisdom stand. All it took, I told myself, to find the linchpin that might give these verses a common bond, would be some prayerful pondering.

More pondering than praying – which is, sorry to say, my style – is what I was doing that week some thirty years ago as I thumbed back and forth through Scripture's pages. The Hebrew lesson was a snippet out of Moses' life when his and God's patience was being stretched to the limits. The supposed "chosen ones" had moved on from just grumbling about how long it was taking to get to that "promised land," to outright rebellion: they fashioned a god of their own.

The story has it that God was incensed. Grousing is one thing, God told Moses, but idolatry is another, and God would have none of it. Had Moses forgotten that that was the first of the big ten? Moses, according to the writer of Exodus, acting like the loving father he presumed God to be, begged God to forgive the children of Israel – give them another chance – and God did just that.

The gospel lesson was from that chapter in Luke where Jesus uses three stories to answer the charge that he not only welcomes unsavory characters, but eats with them as well. We have given the stories names: The Lost Sheep, The Lost Coin, and The Prodigal Son.

Paul wrote the epistle lesson for that long ago week, although there is some question that he did, in fact, write those letters to Timothy. But let's leave proof of authorship to the Biblical scholars, and just listen to these few lines:

"I thank him who has given me strength for this, Christ Jesus our Lord, because he judged me faithful by appointing me to his service, though I formerly blasphemed and persecuted and insulted him; but I received mercy and the grace of our Lord overflowed for me with the faith and love that are in Christ Jesus"

And it was this line from that lesson, "but I received mercy and the grace of our Lord," that gave me my linchpin: grace.

"God's unmerited favor toward us" is the grace definition my seminary professor gave me, and

Marvelous grace of our loving Lord,
Grace that exceeds our sin and our guilt,
Yonder on Calvary's Mount out-poured.
There where the blood of the lamb was spilt.
Grace, grace, God's grace,
Grace that will pardon and cleanse within,
Grace, grace, God's grace,
Grace that is greater than all our sin.

is the singing definition I learned in my growing up years. So, I decided to preach a sermon on grace.

Strange as it may seem, given the popularity of the word in church circles and "Amazing Grace" having become an international hymn, I had never preached a sermon on the subject. Plenty of times in plenty of sermons I had used the word, but at no time had I ever written a whole sermon on grace.

And that wasn't all: I could not find a single sermon on grace in any of the sermon books in my library. Having long felt that preachers ought to read the pulpit masters, I had, over the years, gathered up new and used collections of the likes of Fosdick, Buttrick, Read, Kennedy, Armstrong, and Hamilton; nowhere, in any of them, could I find a complete sermon on grace.

So I began to scribble some notes as to why this might be so, if, indeed it was so, or simply an indication of the limitations of my library. Just suppose, though, that my limited research is on to something – not many whole sermons on grace – doesn't that seem strange? In a time when so many struggle with guilt?

"It's not the feeling of anything I've ever done, which I might get away from, or of anything in me I could get rid of – but of emptiness, of failure, towards someone or something, outside of myself; and I feel I must . . .atone – is that the word?"

I scribbled those lines from T. S. Eliot's, "The Cocktail Party" on my note gathering sheets, as well as a reference to poor Joseph K in Kafka's, The Trial. The poor man stood accused – the charges against him never read – and I jotted him down as possible sermon material – an archetype of our guilted age.

While I was making some other notes – notes about the prevalence of guilt, and Eliot's references to "emptiness" and "failure," trying to get my head around this supposed absence of sermons on grace just when it appears we need the love and acceptance the word implies – the germ of an idea settled in.

It's been so long ago I can't remember which came first, the quote or the idea. Thirty years later, does it really matter? Knowing how my mind works – quotes, poetry lines, stories just seem to pop up – I'll let the quote take precedence. When a ballerina was asked to explain her dance, she replied: "If I could have said it, I wouldn't have needed to have danced it." The idea was not long coming: perhaps grace is too big a word to put into words. The church has known this from the beginning, fashioning symbols and sacraments to express some of its most treasured articles of faith. Oh, we have our wordy creeds, but when we want to really get serious, we pour some water on a head or break a loaf of bread and raise a chalice. Some things are too big for words.

Do you suppose that grace is one of those words that can't be put into words; that it's too big for that; that it needs something else – its own sacrament-like method of expression? That was the conclusion I drew then, and the sacrament-like method of expression I suggested was the story.

Isn't that what Jesus did, I said when I finally took my place in the pulpit that next Sunday? Weren't stories his way of saying something that really couldn't be said? Like the story in Luke 15 that we have misstitled, "The Prodigal Son." If Jesus were titling it, I said, chances are he would have called it something like "The Loving Father" or, maybe even, "The Grace-full Father." Looking at Rembrandt's, *The Return of the Prodigal Son,* it's the fathers loving hands on the shoulders of the wayward son kneeling before him that draw your attention. This well worn story, I suggested, was one of Jesus' grace stories, and, to my mind at least, his favorite.

I told them another grace story that morning. The late Bishop Gerald Kennedy included it in his Lyman Beecher Lectures on preaching at Yale University. Like a lot of other boys he had a paper route; one that required a 3:30 am wake-up call. One blistery, cold, rainy morning he got up, rode his bicycle down to the press room, folded his papers, stuffed them in his delivery bag, and went back outside, wet and shivering. When he got out to the street, there, parked at the curb, was the family Ford. His father got out, helped him put the bicycle in the trunk, and off they rode. This is how Bishop Kennedy put it:

.

"I can remember my feelings as if this had happened yesterday. My father had to go to work each morning and I had no legitimate claim whatsoever upon him for his kindness. I think I came closer to him that morning and I had a more profound understanding of what fatherhood meant than at any other time in my life."

He told that story under a chapter section titled "grace."

My other grace story that long ago morning was one of my own; it was about my older brother. Benton, nine years my senior, diagnosed with muscular dystrophy at a time when little was known of the disease, received no therapy, and died at twenty-seven, spending the last eleven of those years in bed..

Although my mother was the primary care-giver, the rest of us seven children were called upon, at times, to assist her. After my older sisters married and moved away, and my other brother being four years my junior, I inherited the role of primary back-up caregiver.

Sad to say, there were instances when I did not relish this responsibility. Our house, with its large lawn, served as the community's athletic field – the after school gathering place for games – and when Mama would come to the door and shout out, "Thomas, Benton needs you," the grudging steps I sometimes took toward Benton's room let me know that being "my brother's keeper" had its down side.

On such occasions resentment would give way to guilt. Especially when I would remember that my younger brother and I had dodged this genetic bullet. You see, the strain of muscular dystrophy in our family is carried by the women and infects all the male offspring. Why Benton and not Luther and me? Getting called away from a game is no big deal, is it? Not when you have a brother who never gets to play a game.

Occasional dreams let me know that residual guilt was there, even into adulthood. I had not done well as a self-sacrificing, all loving brother, my dream maker told me.

Then one night, just a few years back, I told the congregation, I had a Benton dream. I was in Reagan National Airport in Washington, D. C., rushing to my plane's assigned gate, and, rounding a corner, there sat Benton, directly in front of me, in a wheelchair. All the old feelings of guilt and shame rose to the surface as I stood and looked at him. Here I was, I thought to myself, going somewhere, and, like it had been so often over the years, leaving him behind. Benton looked at me, smiled, and said, simply, "It's okay."

That was my grace story for that sermon. Benton understood. All those years he knew: the feelings – anger, resentment, love, sorrow, joy, even; he knew, and taking me as I was, loved me just the same.

And here's how I wrapped the sermon up:

Grace. Perhaps only a story will do it. Do you have a grace story? If you do, it is better than any sermon on the subject. If you can't think of any, remember the one about God's not letting his idolatrous chosen ones go, or the one about the loving father who welcomed his wastrel son home – with a party. God is like that – tell your self – full of grace, and he loves and accepts us all, just as we are.

Do you have a grace story?

Teach Us To Pray

You can probably count on the fingers of one hand the number of times I have preached on the subject of prayer. Even after I committed myself to preaching on the lectionary there have been precious few times that I dealt with the subject.

Given my religious upbringing, this aversion to my preparing pulpit lessons on prayer might seem a bit strange. Ours was a praying home. Some of my earliest recollections are those mornings when I was awakened hearing my father start his day with a prayer that included the naming of each of his eight children, and asking God to keep an eye on us that day. During those hellish days of homesickness when I went away to college, it was some comfort to know that my Dad was still on his knees every morning praying for Thomas all alone up there in Boston. A tacky, black and silver, glow in the dark, plaque, picturing Jesus praying in the garden, and announcing that "Prayer Changes Things," traveled with us as we moved from house to house. And an early morning radio program that became a staple in the Starnes household featured Edward McHugh singing:

> Ere you left your room this morning, did you think to pray?
> In the name of Christ your Savior,
> Did you sue for loving favor,
> As a shield today?

None of the preachers I listened to seemed to lack interest in churning out sermons on prayer; most of them variations on the Apostle Paul urging us to "pray without ceasing." Being a church going family, as well as a praying family, meant that attendance at the mid-week prayer service was a requirement – a service whose informality and warmth I found comforting, except on those nights when the preacher would have us "pray around the room." So, "both by precept and example," as we say in church circles, I was taught that prayer was a vital and necessary part of any authentic religious life.

And pray I did as a child. Too many times I heard that bad things happened to people who did not behave themselves, and praying was on every list of good behaviors that I was shown. So, I was taking no chances. If I should die before I woke, I didn't want my soul not taken because I hadn't "said my prayers."

When I became a man, however, as Paul told us to do, "I put away childish things." When any notion of a God who might consign our souls to hell because we didn't "say our prayers" no longer took up any space in my statement of faith, I stopped "saying my prayers."

But I did not stop praying. I couldn't. Preaching became my life's calling and praying went with that particular portfolio. To put it as crassly as I can, I was paid to pray. Rotary clubs, new school openings, Job's Daughters' banquets, the list of places I showed up to invoke God's blessing is legion. And, of course, I prayed in church. My pastoral prayers were carefully crafted and written out, making them available to those who, on occasion, would request a copy.

Please do not assume that prayer for me was always a matter of just doing my job – going through the motions. When I opened a session of Congress, after having given a copy in advance to the House Chaplain – to make sure, I suppose, that I wouldn't be advocating the overthrow of the government – I took that privilege seriously, and managed to, as I remember it, remind those representatives of ours, that we were, in fact, a nation under God, and that notion better be in the backs of their minds as they went about this country's business. And on those hundreds of times that I leaned down over the beds of some precious saints of God, and some not so precious saints of God, who were getting ready to cross over to the other side, and asked God to be with them as they set out on this, their final journey, I took that professional duty of mine very seriously, and meant every word I prayed.

It's just that when I was doing all this praying as a part of my job, Tom Starnes wasn't saying his prayers. And, like the Psalmist, my soul was, at times, "disquieted within me," suggesting that we never quite leave our childhoods behind.

It was my head that attempted to rescue my soul and relieve it of its disquietude. Brother Lawrence's *Practicing the Presence* suggested that as we go about our duties – whatever those duties happen to be – we can sense the presence of God in our lives. This was the way it was with him, he wrote; as he toiled amidst the pots and pans in his monastery kitchen, he was, in point of fact, praying. "Neat," I said to myself, "I'm praying as I ride around making calls or sitting in boring trustee meetings."

Bishop John A. T. Robinson joined with Brother Lawrence in calming my prayer conscience. In the chapter on prayer in his book, *Honest to God*, Bishop Robinson suggests, among other things, that whenever he was engaged in meaningful dialogue with someone – seeking, perhaps, to ascertain the mind of God – he was, in fact, praying. "Wow," I said to myself, "not just a few of my days have their share of meaningful dialogue. So, maybe I am more of a prayer than I thought."

Dom Chapman helped with my praying *bona fides*. One day I chanced on this quote of his: "One is praying, or having breakfast, or talking or working, or amusing oneself, but one is principally conscious that one is doing God's will."

Although I accepted the assurances of my head that I was a prayer, my heart just wouldn't be quiet. Maybe I was "practicing the Presence" as I went about my preaching business, but there was no time in my life set aside to go into my closet, as Jesus instructed us to do, close the door, and pour out my heart to the God of my understanding. And it was my heart's raising questions about my praying *bona fides* that kept me from preaching on the subject of prayer unless the lectionary lessons backed me into a corner.

Then one day in early February, during the final decade of my preaching life, praying started its move from my head to my heart, and, in the process, becoming more personal than professional.

My Paul-like "thorn in the flesh" was getting the best of me. Therapy, my old stand-by, wasn't coming through as it had in the past, and the self-help books I obsessively purchased seemed only to mock the depths of my despair with their all too glibly listed steps toward improvement. Then early one morning as I stood at the kitchen sink, pouring down its drain my elixir of choice – a practice that even I knew to be a meaningless ritual – I also poured out my heart to God, and within days I was sitting with a counselor who steered me to a church basement room full of people who talked about getting on their knees each morning and asking God for help. It was this group, through the power of its example, that led me to hope that there just could be something to this praying business, and perhaps Mama's tacky plaque was right, "Prayer Changes Things."

So, I began to make prayer a part of my everyday life. Riding in the car, sitting at work – almost anywhere – I would, quite often, have a go at it with God. Nothing big deal; just maybe an expression of thanks or a request for guidance.

Something else happened to me about this time in my life: grandchildren came to share my days with me, and I found myself more concerned about them than I remembered being about their parents when they were children. So I began asking God to help them as my Dad had asked God to help me. Late one night my wife and I received a call from our daughter telling us that Jacob, one of her twins, was being rushed by ambulance to Children's Hospital in Washington, D. C. The antibiotics weren't working and Jacob was struggling for breath. Shortly after Wave and I arrived at the hospital, the emergency technicians wheeled dear, sweet, little Jacob in. With electrodes pasted to his tiny chest and an IV shunt fastened to one of his little fingers, his eyes were anxiously casing this strange room. The first thing I did after I kissed him was walk over to a corner of the emergency waiting room and ask God to please not let anything happen to this precious life which had been such a gift to us.

Nothing happened to Jacob, and in a few days he was home sleeping soundly in the bed next to his twin sister, Hannah. Does this mean my prayer worked? Who knows? And truth be told, for me, it doesn't really matter. I would hate to think that little children, or anyone else for that matter, gets better or doesn't get better because of our prayers; that God has any control over these things and waits for our prayers to decide what to do about them. No, I don't think whether or not we pray should have anything to do with whether or not prayer works.

In the early eighties I went to hear Frederick Buechner lecture at Virginia Theological Seminary. The three lectures consisted of his reading the three chapters of his soon to be published memoir, *Now and Then*. Midway through the second lecture – having to do with his time on the faculty of Phillips Exeter Academy in New Hampshire – he told of going to hear Agnes Sanford lecture on spirituality. Although, as he said, "spiritual was another of those words that I always choked on a little, and faith-healing was something I associated with charlatans and the lunatic fringe," he went to hear this proponent of faith healing lecture on spirituality, simply because a Jungian analyst friend of his said he ought to.

And he was not disappointed. Agnes Sanford seemed so real – nothing like the charlatan or lunatic he might have imagined.

"Some of what she said I put into *The Final Beast* through a character named Lillian Flagg, but more importantly, when I got back to Exeter, I tried to put it also into practice. Every morning before school began, I would bicycle up Tan Lane to the school church, and there in that shabby old building – all by myself with breakfast coffee still warm in my stomach and trying to empty my mind of the thousand things I would have to start doing when the bell rang for classes – I would kneel in one of the creaking, varnished pews and pray simply for the power to pray, which was a gift of the Holy Spirit promised to us all, Agnes Sanford told us, . . .

"Did they work those early morning prayers with breakfast on my breath? How can you ever be sure? How can you know what you would have been, what you would have done, if you hadn't prayed? . . . Nothing ever happened that I could either see or hear happening. . . . I can say only that I kept on doing it week after week and to a lesser degree, more haphazardly, dimly, without a bicycle, have kept on doing it ever since. Maybe that in itself is the miracle."

Thomas Moore, author of the widely acclaimed book, *Care of the Soul,* said, in a devotional book,

"A billboard near an old house of mine displayed in six-foot type: PRAY, IT WORKS. I always thought this was the ultimate in American pragmatism. If it doesn't work, do you stop praying? What does it mean to say that prayer works? You get what you want? Life gets better?

"My billboard would say: PRAY. IT MAY NOT WORK. . . . Pray – period! Don't expect anything. Or better, expect nothing. Prayer cleanses us of expectations and allows holy will, providence, and life itself an entry. What could be more worth the effort – or the non-effort?"

And yet, when Jesus' disciples up and asked him one day to teach them to pray, his lesson came in three parts. The first was a model prayer – the one you and I still say – that lays some requests at God's feet. The next part is a story that makes the not so hidden suggestion that God works on the principle that it's the squeaky wheel that gets the oil. And the last point in Jesus' lesson is the bold claim that if we ask, we will get; if we seek, we will find; and if we knock, the door will be opened.

Faith bottom lines are hard for me to draw. Especially any final word on prayer. Experience has taught me that a lot of things asked for are not received; a lot of things sought aren't found; and a fair number of doors knocked on are never opened. The same experience, however, has taught me that most of us keep on praying, and asking, like I did when Jacob was sick, and you did, too – maybe doing right now – when someone special to you stood, or stands, in the need of prayer, and hoping, Thomas Moore, notwithstanding, that prayer works.

Bishop Justinian of the Romanian Orthodox Church is reported to have said, "When you pray, don't theologize." Take that bit of high church wisdom and tack on Nike's promotional slogan, "Just Do It," and, for me at least, you get something approaching a prayer bottom line.

STOPPING SHORT

Hidden in one of the early chapters of the faith story that has captured me is a sentence that most Bible readers, I would judge, have probably skipped right over. Its five words close out one of those genealogy passages – a long list of unpronounceable names – which many of us pay little or no attention to as we hurry on to the good parts, or, what we hope will be some good parts, of what came to be called "the greatest story ever told." And had this portion of the 11th chapter of Genesis not been the Hebrew lesson for that long ago Sunday morning, I would have missed it, too.

"And Terah died in Haran." That's the group of words in question. Two proper nouns, a conjunction, a preposition and a verb. That's all. But like so many other things, I dared to assume back then, this sentence was more than the sum of its parts.

You see, Terah was Abram's – later to become Abraham – father. The scripture makes no mention of Terah's faith, giving no indication that his packing his family up and heading toward Canaan's Land was his answering any call from God to head toward that promised territory. What is suggested is that this was nothing more than an early on population movement out of Mesopotamia. However, given the fact that God's call to Abram follows close on the heels of Terah's death notice, it very well might have been God's way of at least getting Abram started on that trek that would eventually lead to the land of promise and Israel's birth as a nation.

But Terah would never set foot on that holy ground. For, as the story says, when they got to a dot on the map – a place called Haran – they made camp for the night and when dawn came they stayed put. Haran became home – the place where Terah died.

Why did this way station become home for Terah – that was the question I attempted to answer in that sermon. There was not much factual information for me to go on – none actually – just a bit of homiletical guesswork.

And my first guess was that the decision to stay put – to make Haran home – was due to changing circumstances. It was an extended family that set out for Canaan. There is no mention of Terah having a wife, but besides Abram and his wife, Sarai, Terah took along his grandson, Lot. Maybe one of them got sick, or it could be that Terah did have a wife, and it was she who decided that the open road was not for her. Circumstances do change things, we have come to say, so maybe that's all there was to Terah's decision.

However, circumstances might have had nothing to do with Terah's decision I went on to suggest, still engaging in a bit of homiletical guesswork. Terah himself might have decided that he had had enough. Even if the two hundred and five years the story credits him with having lived is a bit of a Biblical stretch, chances are he was a very old man, and he simply wanted to settle down. Besides, maybe he liked it there in Haran. The land of Canaan could be all it was made out to be – flowing with milk and honey and possessing all those other added attractions – but nothing wrong with the green grass that he could see growing on this side of the fence.

Here's how I said it back in the day, as we have come to say:

"It's a great day in anyone's life when where they are seems okay; when they look at all they have going for them and decide that the place they are is just fine and they like it. So they stop running and settle down with who they are and where they are. So, I like to think that perhaps Terah fell in love with Haran and decided to stay there until he died."

Being mid-forties, though, and doing a bit of looking at the road that stretched out ahead of me, I came up with another suggestion of why

Terah turned his overnight stay into a permanent dwelling place: this sentence could be a rather short story about settling in too soon – stopping short, maybe.

As was so often the case I wrote a sermon to myself. With two children in college and another one close behind them, still sitting on that long deferred dream of a Ph. D., wondering if being a preacher was the way I wanted to finish out my days here on earth, feeling oh so comfortable in a marvelous church with glorious music, was I "settling in" too soon. Maybe that's what kept Terah in Haran, I suggested.

We do that, I preached; a fair amount of us do. A. J. Cronin's novel, *The Citadel* is about a doctor who stopped dreaming about moving on. One day his wife said:

"Don't you remember how you used to talk about life as an attack upon the unknown, an assault uphill; as though you had a castle up there you could see but could not reach?"

Cronin has the doctor laugh as he says, cynically,

> "I was young then and foolish. That was romantic talk."

We do this, I went on to say, when we settle in. We rationalize or make excuses: our hopes were too ambitious, out of our reach, or didn't square with our abilities. Sometimes this is true; sometimes it isn't.

We best be careful, I concluded, and make sure that our Promised Lands really are unreachable or unrealistic pipe dreams, and not just evidence of a loss of nerve, aversion to risk, or a fear of failure.

Here's what I actually said to end that long ago sermon:

"And Terah died in Haran." I don't know what really happened. It could have been because of altered circumstances – something that he couldn't help. It could have been his own choice – simply because he fell in love with Haran. It could have been the result of his stopping short – of quitting just before he got to his destination. I don't know.

"But does it really matter about him? Isn't the critical issue what's happening with us, in our lives, now: why are we where we are at this point in our lives? And the only reason for us wondering about Terah and why he died in Haran, is so that we might look at ourselves and wonder why we are where we are."

I Never Promised You
a Rose Garden

(This sermon had rather broad appeal given the number of persons who requested a copy. One was a university professor – middle to late fifties – who never offered any feed-back on what I had said. This Sunday was different. He told me that this sermon was one of my best. No way he could have known what was in store for him, although I have lived long enough to keep an open mind about such things. Some months later he died in his sleep. When you finish reading this, I hope you will agree with the decision I made to write it exactly as I preached it thirty-five years ago today – January 21, 1979.)

My preacher brother took me to task over Christmas for spending too much time in a sermon telling how I arrived at my subject. I told him that it had to do with style. I reminded him that Reggie Jackson didn't have to stand at home plate and watch his line shot soar out over the fences before starting his jog around the bases; but his standing there, motionless, savoring that moment – that's style. Johnny Carson, I went on, doesn't have to fake a golf swing to signal the end of his monologue. It's style.

Even as I defended myself, I knew my little brother was on to something. So, I resolved to work on it – forgo this particular homiletic "style" of mine – and just stand up each Sunday and let her fly. And if you have been paying attention over the past weeks you will have noted that that is precisely what I have done.

No One Knows When It's a Good Day

And I fully intended to do that today. However, I can't. You see, I'm afraid some of you might read the announced sermon topic in our Saturday Washington Post ad, and have come this morning expecting to hear me say something about the subject, "I Never Promised You a Rose Garden." So, I can't just stand up here and "damn the torpedoes, full speed ahead." You need a bit of an explanation.

First, though, I ought to tell you what I was going to do with the topic. You probably remember it as a pop song from a few years back. I don't remember who sang it, but it went like this:

> I beg your pardon,
> I never promised you a rose garden.

Before it was a song, it was a book – a book about the treatment of a young girl at a psychiatric hospital in neighboring Rockville, Maryland. The girl had lived a tortured life and was trying to overcome with the aid of a skilled therapist, who wouldn't let her give in by giving up. After all, the doctor was telling her, nobody ever said life was a garden of roses; none of us is promised that.

That was to be my starting point: that life was never promised as something all neat and nice and beautiful; life has its scary side; evil is real; tragedy is all a part of our sojourn here on earth; every home will, one day, have its hush. No one has promised us a rose garden.

Not even God. I had written down in my notes, and planned to quote the song that Debbie, Ellen and Floyd sang in the youth service a few Sundays back. Remember it:

> God hath not promised skies always blue,
>   Flower strewn pathways all our lives through.
> God hath not promised sun without rain,
>   Joy without sorrow, peace without pain.

I wanted to say this – especially this – because we Christians tend to think that following God should guarantee a pain-free existence and that if sorrow comes a stalking then we must have sinned or something else has gone terribly wrong. Even God can't promise us a rose garden is something I knew I would have to say.

When I got to this point in my preparation the second thoughts about this subject started. This is awfully close to what I had to say to you just last week, I told myself; even though I do think there is more to say on the subject than what I said then. Especially this all too prevalent idea among us God-followers that the good life is the trouble free life; that somehow the greatest gift to us from a benevolent deity would be life as a rose garden; green, deep red, fragrant, with a necessary thorn or two, but not too many and none too sharp.

We really think this way, don't we? Trouble and suffering shouldn't be, and if they raise their ugly heads in our lives, we have to turn them into some good; that this is what Paul meant when he penned those words in the 8th chapter of Romans – words about all things working together for some good for those who trusted – and that God's will for us is to turn every minus into a plus, and every storm cloud into a rainbow. So, churches are full on Easter and only partially full on Maundy Thursday and Good Friday, and we Methodists go so far as to leave "he descended into hell" out of the Apostle's Creed when we affirm it.

I wanted to talk about this compulsive wish of ours to try and make all things work together for some good, as Paul put it. I wanted to drive home the point that God hasn't promised us a trouble free existence or a pain-free world; that some things are evil and wrong and tragic and will never be anything else. And however strong our faith, or however deep our commitment, some things in our lives will never be anything but thorns. There is no way that the slaughter of 6 million Jews will ever "work together for some good." I don't care how long it takes the sands of time to dribble through existence's hour glass, that dark splotch on history's pages will always be there, as evil and not as good. And in my own piece of history, my older brother's muscular dystrophy and death at 27 will never be anything other than tragic and wasteful. That handsome face and brilliant mind – twisted and wasted. Oh, there was some good, but not nearly enough.

Don't get me wrong. This in no way means I think life is rotten or void of meaning or that God is cruel. Not at all. God may not have promised us a rose garden under skies always blue, but God did give us a promise. So I wanted to include this in the sermon and be sure to quote the chorus of the song I just mentioned – the one the kids sang a few weeks back in their service:

> But God hath promised strength for the day,
> Rest for the labor, light for the way.
> Grace for the trials, help from above,
> Unfailing kindness, undying love.

And I especially wanted to emphasize this as what I see as the Christian's approach to evil and tragedy – not a denial of it by trying to turn it into some good – but a facing of it, head on, and accepting it as a part of life; knowing – at least trusting – that God would be there by your side as together you walked through this particular valley.

Although I feel strongly about this subject, I hesitated to deal with it since I would be traveling in the same territory that I wandered around in last week.

Truth be told, however, this wasn't what kept me from going ahead with this week's announced topic. It was fear that got the best of me – a fear that I couldn't put into words what I believe about this whole question of good and evil. When it comes time for me to say something about this age old question, I'm like the man who said to Jesus one day, "Lord, I believe; help my unbelief." Some say so easily that God wills it. Those words have never crossed my lips, and yet I have long felt that the Persian proverb, "all sunshine makes a desert" is on to something; that sometimes, in those dark and dismal moments in our lives, we have sensed a presence that has made all the difference. It is a plank in my creedal platform that the dark side of life seems to be necessary for our growth, and in some instances, our hurting helps. But how do I stand up here and say that without sounding sick.

So, I was afraid to go ahead with the subject. Not only was I afraid I couldn't say what I mean – because I really don't know for sure what

I mean – there was also a fear of rejection. You see, this is a time for answers and clear cut statements of faith and success stories in the church. The churches that are growing and the religious movements that are really on the move are those who promise answers and give them, as well as rolling out statements of belief that hold out the hope of physical and material health. These success obsessed communities of faith do not talk a lot about questions and doubts, and if prosperity and healing doesn't come about, then somebody's faith failed. There isn't a lot of talk about meaningless tragedy and suffering. For them, if you look hard enough, you can find God's hand in all things, giving it some purpose and allowing it to work together for some good.

When I thought, then, about standing here and saying God never promised us a rose garden; that evil and tragedy are facts of life; and not everything that happens has meaning or turns out okay, well, I really didn't want to say any of that, not today, anyway.

Even though I had a text for it. It's a familiar one, even to us Methodists, not known for our Biblical literacy. John wrote it: "The light shines in the darkness, and the darkness has not overcome it." The darkness is there, without doubt, for all of us at one time or another. It's real; it doesn't leave. But it is brightened by God's light.

Well, that's what I thought about saying, and you know something? I have always been afraid that some Sunday I just might spend so much time telling you what I was going to say, that I wouldn't have enough time left to say it.

And it finally happened. I promise you, though, that I will re-visit this subject again, some day. Until that time, remember the title – we were never promised a rose garden – and a little of what I said about my reluctance to preach on the subject. That will have to do for now.

The Courage of One's Doubts

When the long time CBS television commentator, Eric Sevareid, died in the summer of 1992, the Washington Post printed excerpts from his final Evening News commentary broadcast in November, 1977, giving me my text for the next Sunday's sermon. Here's what the Post said Mr. Sevareid had said when he signed off for the last time:

"Mine has been an unelected, unlicensed, un-codified office and function. The rules are self-imposed. These were a few: not to underestimate the intelligence of the audience and not to overestimate its information; to elucidate when one can more than advocate; . . .to retain the courage of one's doubts as well as one's convictions in this world of dangerously passionate certainties."

Doubt has not been treated kindly within these stained glass walls over the years. There have been more than just a few who have gone so far as to call doubt a sin. Most, though, have stopped short of tacking on the sin label, and been satisfied with calling it a failure of faith. There have, on occasion, been some voices raised to speak a good word or two on behalf of doubt. Tennyson comes to mind.

> "There lives more faith in honest doubt, believe me, than in half the creeds."

This is a line he stuck in his poem, "In Memoriam." For the most part, however, it's conviction that we people of faith have lauded.

Conviction also plays well outside these sanctuaries of ours. It's the people who take stands, know what they believe, and have the courage to act on those beliefs, that we admire. When we are on the look-out for leaders, the last thing we want to find is someone who, as we say, "waffles."

> I am not for free trade, and I am not for protection,
> I approve of them both and to both have objection;
> In going through life I increasingly find
> It's a terrible nuisance to make up your mind;
> So, in spite of all pressures, reproaches, predictions,
> I firmly adhere to unsettled convictions."

Anyone who wants to lead us, we say, better be able to tell us where they stand on the issues, and the plan they have in mind to move our ship of state on down the road (to deliberately mix metaphors). Those who come looking for our vote better have a carefully worked out agenda, and an obviously steely spine that when they are backed into a political corner they will have the courage of their convictions.

And there's nothing wrong with these great expectations. Convictions are good things to have, necessary even, and also the courage to go with them. There is a story about the German poet, Heinrich Heine, who was standing one day with a friend in front of the Cathedral of Amiens, France. "Tell me, Heinrich," said his friend, "why can't people build piles like this anymore?" "My dear friend," Heine replied, "in those days people had convictions. We moderns have opinions. And it takes more than an opinion to build a gothic cathedral."

Yes, it does, and we shouldn't – we can't – live full lives without convictions.

But, we also can't live without doubts – at least not honestly – with our hearts and minds open. Reinhold Niebuhr, a major theological voice of the twentieth century, and still being read, wrote, "There was a time in my life when I had all the answers. My real growth began when I discovered that the questions to which I had the answers were not the important questions." Which calls to mind Elie Wiesel's comment that most of life's good questions remain unanswered, suggesting, at least to me, that given our kind of world, those who want to live responsibly will have to live with the courage of their doubts. And, as the poet, Rilke, reminds us, "Be patient toward all that is unsolved in your heart and try to love the questions themselves."

Because the questions – the unanswerable questions – can suggest that a lot of life is beyond us, and none of us possesses the whole truth.

Stephen Vincent Benet wrote an epic poem titled John Brown's Body in which he has Abraham Lincoln say:

> They come to me and talk about God's will
> Day after day, laymen and ministers,
> All of them are sure they know God's will.
> I am the only man who does not know it.

There are those among us, even now as in Lincoln's day, who profess to know God's will on the issues that not only trouble us, but are threatening to tear us apart as a society. Most of us know, though – at least I hope enough of us know – deep down, that life isn't that simple, and what we need, as Eric Sevareid suggested, is the "courage of our doubts in a world of dangerously passionate certainties."

One other thing: in this kind of world, where absolute certainly is rarely an option, if we are ever going to act, it will be because we have such courage. Harry Emerson Fosdick, of Riverside Church, New York, fame, who in the mid-twentieth century gave voice to an evangelical liberalism (yes, there is such a thing) said in one of his sermons: "But in every realm where truth is sought, the hour comes when further discovery depends not on argument, but on experiment." "You stick your toe in the water," as the old Hebrew legend put it; it's only then that the sea parts and makes a way for you to cross.

Sheldon Kopp in his book, *The Hanged Man,* recounts this ancient Hasidic tale:

"A woman came to Rabbi Israel, the maggid of Koznitz, and told him, with many tears, that she had been married a dozen years and still had not borne a son. "What are you willing to do about it?" he asked her. She did not know what to say.

"My mother," so the maggid told her, "was aging and still had no child. When she heard that the holy Baal Shem was stopping over in Apt, in the course of his journey, she hurried to his inn and begged him to pray that she might bear a son.

"What are you willing to do about it," the holy Baal Shem asked the maggid's mother? "My husband is a poor bookbinder," she replied, "but I do have one fine thing that I shall give to the rabbi."

She went home as fast as she could and fetched her good cape which was carefully stored away in a chest. But when she returned to the inn with it, she heard that the Baal Shem had already left for Mezbizh. She immediately set out after him and since she had no money to ride, she walked from town to town with her cape, until she came to Mezbizh. The Baal Shem took the cape and hung it on the wall. "It is well," he said. My mother walked all the way back, from town to town, until she reached Apt. A year later I was born.

"I, too," cried the woman, "will bring you a good cape of mine so that I may get a son."

"That won't work," said the maggid. "You heard the story. My mother had no story to go by.'

The Nativity's Naiveté

(This is another sermon that I am leaving the way I preached it on December 21, 1986.)

It was the week before Christmas and I had been standing in the post office line for some time. When I finally reached the front of that line I asked for 100 Christmas stamps. The woman behind the barricade asked, "Religious?" I laughed and answered, "What other kinds of Christmas stamps are there? Christmas is religious." She tried to explain – like I was from another planet – and I did not interrupt. She even showed me some of the pagan options.

A non-religious Christmas? I remembered an old Peanuts comic strip. I still have it filed away. Baltimore Sun, December 23, 1962. Lucy, Linus and Charlie Brown are toddling off to school. Lucy says:

"This is 'show and tell' day at school, isn't it? Rats! I forgot to bring something. Did you remember that this was 'show and tell' day, Linus?"

Linus speaks: "Yes, I have a couple of things here to show the class. These are copies I've been making of some of the Dead Sea Scrolls. See? This is a duplicate of a scroll of Isaiah, chapters 38 to 40. It was made from seventeen pieces of sheepskin, and was found in a cave by a shepherd.

"Here I've made a copy of the earliest known fragment ever found. It's a portion of I Samuel 23:9-16. I'll try to explain to the class how these manuscripts have influenced modern scholars."

Lucy says: "Very interesting."

Linus responds: "I thought it might be at least faintly appropriate to the season. Are you bringing something for 'show and tell' Charlie Brown?"

Poor Charlie Brown – standing there all the while, with this little squiggly line on his forehead, says: "Well, I had a little red fire engine here, but I think maybe I'll just forget it."

A non-religious Christmas? I don't see how. You can declare public places off limits for crèches. Schools can opt for "Jolly Old St. Nicholas" in lieu of "Joy to the World," and the U. S. Postal Service can offer you a choice of stamps – with Jesus or without. But we know; how do you spell Christmas? You spell it C-H-R-I-S-T.

I can tell I'm getting back into the swing of things because the old homiletical feelers are at work. Folks, you ought to be kind to us preachers. It isn't easy facing, essentially, the same group of people week in and week out, and coming up with fresh material that will challenge, instruct, comfort, chide, and, yes, even entertain. So the preacher who cares about preaching is constantly on the prowl for sermon material. You can't ever have too many good sermon ideas.

My "homiletical feelers" were put on hold, sort of, during my recent term as district superintendent. I had other things to do, and, since I didn't preach every Sunday, and when I did preach, it was a different congregation each time, so I could do a bit of sermonic re-cycling. But I knew I was getting back into preaching shape the other morning at Sherrill's Bakery as I was reading the sports section of the Washington Post.

Yes, I read – I devour – the sports pages. Yes, horrors, I read them first. I used to say, in my defense, that Chief Justice Earl Warren always read the sports section first, but I don't defend myself anymore.

Anyway, I was deep into my sports reading, and there, in an article about the trouble one of our United Methodist schools is in with the NCAA over code violations, my homiletical feeler touched something.

The school is Southern Methodist University, in Dallas, Texas, and it is accused of cheating in recruiting its athletes, among other things.

Well, Perkins Theological Seminary is on the campus of SMU and the faculty there is steamed. "What's this: a Wesleyan school with strong United Methodist roots, cheating?" The article ends with this quote from Dr. Leroy Home, professor of pastoral theology and president of the faculty senate. Dr. Home said:

"John Wesley would say that what is going on here is very self-centered. Narcissistic. He would think it's sinful and shameful that an educational institution would encourage people to learn more, solely to earn more. His philosophy was not anti-business. He said earn all you can, save all you can, to give all you can. But not to tailbacks! Mr. Wesley might have said, my doctrine of sin has always been strong, but I'm revising it downward.

"On the flip side he would say, as depraved as humans are, there is always the possibility of transformation. Our tradition is, if anything, a bit of naïve optimism. Conversion is always possible. There is always the possibility that the town drunk will walk to the altar and be a changed man, and, when he does, he will be fully accepted. The football program here, I'm afraid, is the town drunk."

My homiletical feeler beeped when it hit that phrase, "a bit of naïve optimism.

There is that in our Methodist heritage. At one time or another we have felt that we could "win the world for Christ," or, short of doing that, we could at least kill off old "Demon Rum" here in the states. Ours has been a naïve optimism fueling our faith: that if we worked hard enough, studied long enough, prayed sincerely enough, we could overcome.

But, my homiletical feeler was working on Christmas, and the "naïve optimism" phrase led me there.

Take Isaiah, the Hebrew lesson for this morning. Can you read it without thinking something on the order of "naïve optimism?" Deserts blossoming as roses. Eyes of the blind being opened; ears of the deaf being unstopped; lame men leaping like deer; people who can't speak, singing for joy; not to mention the complete absence of any ravenous beasts.

And Luke's nativity account, the gospel lesson for today. Come on now. When you think of it, how naive can you get? Talk about a story that won't play, even in Peoria. You see, there's this poor young maiden whom no one has ever heard of, and this equally poor, non-descript carpenter. Well, God told the young girl that she would give birth to a baby and that baby would . . . .Come on now. Shepherds, stars, angels, stable, how naïve can you get?

That's how I came upon the title: The Nativity's Naiveté. Now let me rescue a word. When you think of something being naïve, what comes to mind? Uninformed? Probably. Gullible? That, too. As in when we say, "Oh, you're so naïve, you'd believe anything." Well, those who keep us straight on words – the Websters and the Rogets – don't put naivete anywhere near stupidity or gullibility. When they talk about the word they use such synonyms as "simplicity of nature," "unsophisticated," "innocent," "open," "ingenuous."

The naïve optimism of Christmas: well, you have some very simple folk believing that God does come through as promised. You have some unsophisticated peasants who are open to what they perceive to be the will of God and are quite willing to rise up and follow; they are so artlessly simple that they know they don't know everything, making them open to the discovery of truth.

The naïve optimism of Christmas: you have some very simple, unsophisticated people who know, first hand, that rulers can be tyrants and suffering is real, who nonetheless, believe that "in thy dark streets shineth the everlasting light."

You see, the naiveté of the Nativity is not pretending that things aren't as bad as they seem. It is rather, as Reinhold Niebuhr reminded us, "always an ultimate optimism which has entertained all the facts" which can lead to pessimism, but, for the believer, does not, because the believer's hope is in God and however dark the night, morning is on the way. They may not live to see it, according to Niebuhr. It may take centuries, and they, like Moses, may die before the Promised Land is reached. But God's word is sure, and they know whom they have believed and are persuaded that God is able, to quote an old hymn of the church. I read somewhere that Henrik Ibsen's last word was "nevertheless." That's a great word for Christians. This is the way it is – nevertheless. It's a great Christmas word. "Unto us a child is born, unto us a son is given." Nevertheless.

Christmas 1986. What about the naïve optimism of Christmas now, in our time?

The December issue of the Washingtonian magazine featured an article whose gist can be discovered with just a hurried glance at the magazine's cover. In big bold letters you see, "God is Back." In smaller letters you read, "To restore something lost, . . .to find some peace. . .Washingtonians are returning to religion." Inside, there are paragraph headings such as "Churches are an answer to a secular world that is losing faith in the future," "The substitutes for religion have proved thin gruel," and "The Mayflower Van generation wants some Plymouth Rocks." Then comes this wrap up paragraph:

"That hunger, I suspect, is unquenchable – not a hunger only for ceremony and tradition, but a hunger through the ceremony and tradition for the whole mystery and culture that churches and temples represent. They lead us into our innermost selves – maybe that's the first good of them – but they lead us also into the fabric of our civilization, into the awful wars fought in God's name and the wonderful miracles said to have been performed in that same name. They lead to Sir Thomas More, through the eternal string of saints and popes, to Abraham and Isaac, to Moses, to a carpenter's son born under extraordinary circumstances long ago in a land called Galilee. Or so the story goes."

And so it goes. Still as it always has gone. A generation comes and thinks it knows everything there is to know; turns its back on the church. So naïve, those believers and those stories. It may have been good enough for Mom and Dad – that old time religion – but not for us. We are the now generation.

And so it goes. They leave. But they never go too far away, and their wayside altars closely resemble the mainline altars they have left, as well as their symbols and their songs.

And so it goes. In some far country – but never too far – they come to themselves. And the naïve optimism of their religious heritage begins to make some sense to them as they edge their way back home, knowing now that they don't know everything; that the answers to life's real questions aren't in some computer bank somewhere.

And so it goes. And to those who seek – to those who are open – to those who are artlessly simple – naïve, really – the Nativity's naiveté begins to make all the sense in the world.

How silently, how silently, the wondrous gift is given.
So God imparts to human hearts
The blessings of his heaven.
No ear may hear his coming,
But in this world of sin,
Where meek (naïve?) souls will receive him still
The dear Christ enters in.

A Very Present Help

Gregory Bateson said once, "I'll believe computers can think when you ask one a question and it replies: 'That reminds me of a story.'"

Stories do seem to be so much a part of who we are, and, I suppose, a large part of what it means to be human, and to think. I do know that we wouldn't have much to build our faith on if we didn't have our stories. And I love it when the lectionary turns up a story or two for us to read again. Two of the lessons for this Sunday are stories.

The Hebrew lesson is an old one; from a time way back when our faith community was little more than a gleam in God's eye. It's about a Dad and his boys.

Jacob had twelve sons, and Joseph was his favorite. The story says he liked Joseph best because he was the child of his old age.

Such things like that happen. My older sisters say that my brother, Luther, and I were Daddy's favorites. We were numbers seven and eight – the end of a rather long line – and, according to my sisters, Daddy doted on the two of us.

The way I lived the story, though, Luther was my Dad's Joseph. All the old pictures are of him and his blasted curly blond hair. There are no baby pictures of me. There was one picture of me as a toddler in Mama's things when we sorted them all out after her death. I'm standing in front of Nannie Cowan's house in Tennessee; my diaper is drooping down around my knees, and I'm holding a cat. I swear that the focus of that picture is not me but Tabby.

My little brother, like Joseph, was Daddy's favorite. He got the dimes my Dad collected in his little Sussex Trust bank – dimes used to help pay for his college textbooks. He walked off with the family car – a many colored coat equivalency in my eyes. Yeah, I can relate to this story.

A story about a little brother who knows it all; a tattle-tale, too: runs back to Daddy with a negative performance review about his brothers' shepherding skills. It's no wonder his older brothers wanted to drop him in a well.

Fred Craddock says that preachers ought to preach on the Biblical stories more often, and, he says, when he is preparing to preach on one of our faith stories, he gets himself a sheet of paper, and writes across the top of it, "so what."

What is the "so what" of this old story about Joseph and his brothers? Is it what I have been talking about – these family feelings that can, on occasion, run murderously deep?

Oscar Wilde told a story about a Lucifer who was crossing the Libyan Desert when he happened upon some imps who were tormenting a holy hermit. The imps were obviously inexperienced and making no headway in tempting the man of God. Lucifer watched them flounder for a while and then gave them a pointer on the art of temptation

"What you do is too crude. . . . Permit me for one moment." With that he whispered to the holy man: "Your brother has just been made Bishop of Alexandria," and with that a scowl of malignant jealousy clouded the serene face of the hermit. "That," said the devil to his imps "is the sort of thing which I should recommend."

It is an old feeling, old as humankind is old, and it breaks out of families and splits societies and countries, even. But is it the "so what" of this story? I don't think so.

Simply, because of the way the story ends.

Most of us know the rest of the story. Joseph gets out of the pit, and is sold as a slave to a caravan of Ishmaelites. They take him to Egypt and Potiphar's wife has him thrown in jail because he won't fool around with her. In jail he discovers his dream interpreting gifts, and because of that he ends up as head of all Egypt. It is in that position that he meets his brothers again. After toying with them a bit, he lets them know who he is, and they are reconciled.

However, the brothers aren't all that sure about the little twerp: whether after Daddy dies he will do unto others as they have done unto him. So, when Daddy does die, and the boys all gather, the brothers cook up this story about their Dad's death bed plea that Joseph forgive them. Here's how the story ends:

"Joseph wept when they spoke to him. Then his brothers also wept, fell down before him, and said, 'we are here as your slaves.' But Joseph said to them, 'Do not be afraid! Am I in the place of God? Even though you intended to do harm to me, God intended it for good. . . .'"

Isn't that the "so what" of this story: that God is at work in the world; deism is a crock; God has a master plan and is right up to his/her elbows in it all? Frederick Buechner has this line or two in his book, <u>The Clown in the Belfry</u>: "Either life is holy with meaning, or life doesn't mean a damn thing. You pay your money and you take your choice." My best guess is that the "so what" of this story is that God is there, in all of it, the good, the bad, the ugly, and somehow, by God's grace, all of it has a possibility of working together for some good, as the apostle Paul put it.

In a thoughtful book, <u>Sacred Stories of the Ordinary</u>, a rabbi says, "I counsel my students on the eve of their graduation from rabbinic school, all terrified that they won't get the job they want: 'Relax, because God is going to put you where God wants you, whether you like it or not.'"

I think we have to move past trying to settle the argument of how suffering comes about, or why bad things happen to good people, or where God is in all of this. None of our faith stories ever settle this question or give us anything approaching a bottom line. The best we have are stories like the one for today – where some bad things happened to a pretty decent sort – and in spite of that God used it for some good.

In Hemingway's *Farewell to Arms* there is this line: "The world breaks everyone, and then some become stronger at the broken places." Which calls to mind some lines from Leonard Cohen's *Anthem:*

Ring the bells that still can ring,
> Forget your perfect offering.
> There is a crack in everything,
> That's how the light gets in.

Joseph's way of saying it was, "You meant it for evil, but God meant it for good." The "so what" of this story, for me, is that God is there, in our lives, helping us let it all work together for some good.

Riding Out the Storm

For a lot of these ancient Biblical stories my introduction to them came by way of the hymns we sang in church. Take the story Mark tells about the time Jesus calmed the stormy waters that were tossing the boat around that he and his disciples were in, with a simply stated "Peace be still." This story put to music was a favorite of those non-audition required choirs I grew up listening to.

> Master the tempest is raging,
>   The billows are tossing high.
> The sky is oe'r shadowed with blackness,
>   No shelter or help is nigh;
> Carest Thou not that we perish?
>   How canst Thou lie asleep;
> When each moment so madly is threatening
>   A grave in the angry deep.

And then those untrained voices would soft pedal it a bit, and, as I remember it, rather movingly make the pronouncement that

> The winds and the waves shall obey Thy will,
>   Peace, be still, peace be still,

And my boyhood ears heard that those winds and waves did indeed obey Jesus' command that day, and the assurance I was supposed to receive was that wherever the Lord is, there is safety.

You may have grown up in a church that had better music than the one that nurtured me in the faith, but I imagine that this story from

Mark about Jesus calming the storm got the same spin put on it in your church as it did in mine: our Lord has power to calm troubled waters. He was indeed a miracle worker, and, for that matter, still is. So do not be afraid. Given enough faith, all those storms that come blowing into our lives can be calmed. Jesus can say to our storms the same thing he said to that storm back then: "Peace, be still."

There is a story that has made its rounds among us preacher types that has Queen Victoria riding in her royal yacht on the Irish Sea, and they encountered one of those storms that seem to come out of nowhere all of a sudden, bouncing her yacht around on the troubled waters as if it were a toy. When they finally made it safely to port Queen Victoria said to her physician who was travelling with her, "Go up at once, Sir James, and give the admiral my compliments and tell him that that thing must not occur again."

Jesus, for some of us son of God, Messiah, for still others High Admiral of the seas of life, can, with a word, cause our life storms to cease. That is here in this story. "Who then is this that even wind and sea obey him?" And I have no intention of denying the miracle aspects of this story.

But I do want to suggest that perhaps – just perhaps – there might be another word here for us in this ancient story: a truer word – a gospel word. A word that has more to do with calm in the midst of the storm than after it passes; a word about a peace that, as the scriptures put it, "passes all understanding" simply because it occurs in the midst of the turbulence rather than when all the storm clouds have lifted.

That's here in this story, isn't it? Maybe it wasn't Mark's point when he sat down to recount this incident in Jesus' life. It could be that the miracle of the calming of the seas was just a further attempt of Mark to make the sale that Jesus was the promised Messiah. That could be all there is to this story for Mark But isn't there at least a hint of something more?

It's in the master's behavior. Did you miss it? The storm was raging and Jesus was asleep – like a baby. The disciples were busily checking out the exits, trying to spot the flotation collars and he was snoring away.

Absorbed in themselves, as seemed to be the case a good deal of the time, they saw this as him not giving a rap about their welfare. It wasn't that; he was resting in the Lord.

> At the heart of the cyclone tearing the sky
> And flinging the clouds and towers by
> Is a place of central calm;
> In the hollow of God's palm.

That's Edwin Markham helping make my point: that in the midst of storms God's peace can come, and that, in itself, is a miracle.

Like the children of Israel carrying around with them Joseph's bones, over the years I have carried along with me notebooks of quotes and folders of clippings. One of those clippings, yellowed with age, is a column by William Buckley, titled, "On the Death of Charles Pinkney Luckey."

Charles Luckey was a congregational minister, who, at the age of fifty, was stricken with a rare disease that attacked the nerve endings and was a quick killer. Luckey was a jogger, a biker, in perfect health until that day when he couldn't keep his balance on his bike. Buckley writes:

"They took him to Columbia Presbyterian in New York to 'confirm' the diagnosis. One suspects the real reason for the trip was to give the medical students a chance to examine someone suffering from such an exotic disease. . . . It was only there that he yielded to depression as they poked about and asked him questions.

"Before, and after, he was obstinately cheerful and affectionate, dictating to his secretary every day letters of farewell to his friends, letters exalted by a curious dignity that attached to him even as a teenager. He preached his last sermon, propped up by his 17 year old son at the lectern, on the Sunday before Christmas.

"The crisis came shortly after. He called his secretary and dictated a paragraph which he sent to a few friends, and was pronounced by the retired, aged chaplain of Yale University 'the most moving credo to the Christian faith written in my lifetime."

Calm in the midst of the storm – to me that is, not only the true miracle, but the authentic gospel word.

For me it seems a pity that this story has the miracle of the calmed seas in it, simply because it can suggest to us that perhaps in our stormy situations God can work some magic and make everything turn out all right; that with a word from the Almighty our storms can be calmed, and it will be smooth sailing from here on in.

But life isn't like that, even for the faithful. No one knew this better than our Lord. Seas around him were never smooth; storm clouds were always hovering over his head; and on his last day here on earth, when his skies were the blackest, his final words were, "Father, into thy hands I commit my spirit." Calm in the midst of the storm, that, to me is the true gospel miracle.

St. Theresa wrote in the front of her prayer book,

> Let nothing disturb thee,
> Nothing affright thee:
> All things are passing;
> God never changeth;

"But Jesus was in the stern, asleep on the cushion; . . ."

SLENDER THREADS

I had fully intended to leave these Old Testament stories and head on over into the land of Gospels and Epistles. But, as I told you early on, I have this mild addiction to these old, old stories.

Today's is one of the most familiar. In any kind of association test given, and the word Moses appears, chances are that the word "bull rushes" would come to mind. I know the later versions call them reeds, but when most of us here were learning this story those reeds were called bull rushes.

Moses' mother put him in a basket there among those reeds because the Pharaoh at the time was a despotic sort and feared for his reign. You see the Israelites were taking seriously God's command to be "fruitful and multiply." He first tried to get the midwives to kill these new born sons, but they, fearing God's anger, made up a story about the toughness of the Israelite women. So Pharaoh took matters into his own hands and put out the word that all new born males should be killed. So Moses mother put her new born son in a papyrus basket and placed it among the reeds along the river. Moses sister stood at a distance to see what would happen.

Pharaoh's daughter came down to the river to bathe and saw the baby in the basket. She surmised that it must be one of the Hebrew children. Moses' sister, who had been standing nearby, suggested that she would go and get a Hebrew woman to nurse the infant. Pharaoh's daughter thought that a good plan and Moses sister took him to his mother who nursed him until it was time for him to be weaned, and then returned him to Pharaoh's daughter who "took him as her son." It was she who named him Moses, which means, "I drew him out of the water."

A persistent theme of these early-on faith stories of ours is how God moves in mysterious ways – there God is, behind the scenes, orchestrating events so that they fit into some divine scheme of things.

So here you have Moses, who, according to the story, is God's chosen one to lead his people out of bondage and set them on the way to the Promised Land, and he gets placed in Pharaoh's house.

What came to mind as I read this story for the umpteenth time – skimmed it really, because I know it so well – is a book I read a few years back. It's titled, *Between Heaven and Earth.* The author is Robert Johnson, who has lived a fascinating life and this book is a memoir.

Early on he tells of two principles that have guided his life. One is what he calls "The Golden World." He means by this, living with some notion of the world being infected with a heavenly quality. The other principle is what he refers to as "slender threads." Let me let him tell us what this means. He says:

> It is an audacious notion to put forth in this age of science and willful determination that one's existence is somehow inspired, guided, and even managed by unseen forces outside our control. Whether called fate, destiny, or the hand of God, slender threads are at work bringing coherence and continuity to our lives.
>
> What are these slender threads? Being in a particular place at just the right time, meeting someone who steers you in an unforeseen direction, the unexpected appearance of work or money or inspiration just when they are most needed. These are the mysterious forces that guide us and shape who we are."

No One Knows When It's a Good Day

Slender threads: something, someone coming along at just the right time, like Pharaoh's daughter coming down to the river to bathe, and life is never the same. And that's what I want to talk about with you.

The slender thread stories I grew up with came to mind. Daddy didn't call them slender threads. For him it was all God at work. But, I'll get to that.

My dad was a drunk, plain and simple. He was a good man. An honorable man, but he couldn't get his life together and booze played no small part in his inability to make his life work. And the Depression certainly didn't help. He couldn't get steady work. He tried everything: farming, selling Watkins home products door to door. We kept moving, one time living in one of my granddad Starnes' run down tenant houses, which is the house I came home to from the hospital.

And the kids kept coming. Finally, he got a job at the local cement plant as an apprentice machinist. (The slender thread is on its way.) Shortly after that he gets saved, born again I prefer to call it, at a revival meeting in a little church that was across the street from where we were living at the time. (The slender thread is growing.) My brother, Luther, child number eight, is born.

Then one day, quite out of the blue, a notice appears on the cement plant bulletin board. It says that DuPont, in a place called Delaware, is looking for workers – now hear this – especially machinists. I have very early memories of all of us gathered around a dining room – or was it a kitchen – table looking at an atlas. Delaware was 1000 miles away was the distance we came up with.

And we went. A whole new life began. Luther Williams, Hoyt Copeland and all those other drinking buddies were left behind in Tennessee. It was a fresh start for my Dad. Brother Boggs, pastor of the Wilmington, Delaware, Church of the Nazarene, another part of the slender thread, was at the train station to meet us. And he stayed by our side, what with us being, as they put it, "new Christians."

Slender threads – from as far back as I can remember, I have been told that one should expect them.

And some have come along the way for me. When I was little more than ten years old, a traveling evangelist came through our town for the fall revival and scared the bejeebers out of me with a sermon on the unpardonable sin. I had no idea what I could possibly have done, but I knew I had. And I was petrified. Mama and Daddy had a smallish library, and one day, just by chance, I picked up a little book titled, *Impressions*. And in it was a word that seemed written just for me.

There have been so many other instances: people who came into my life: professors, doctors, therapists, and just plain old common people, many of whom sat out in those pews in front of me over the years, who, at some point in my life served as one of Dr. Johnson's slender threads.

Frederick Buechner is one of my favorite writers. He makes a place in his life for these chance happenings – these things I am calling slender threads. He seems to lay them all at or very near the feet of God. Not in any self-righteous way, or in any way that seems to indicate that he knows for sure that God had a hand in it. Here's how he put it in one of his books,

> If God speaks to us at all other than through such official channels as the Bible and the church, then I think that he speaks to us largely through what happens to us."

In one of his books he tells about seeing one of these so-called vanity license plates with just the word "trust" printed on it. He spotted that license plate at one of the darkest moments in his life – his life was in the pits.

As it turned out, it was, as he thought it might be, the plates of a trust officer in a bank, but for Buechner, it was a word from God he needed to hear. And years later, after Buechner had written about it, the banker showed up and gave him the plate, which, as Buechner writes,

Sits propped up on a bookshelf in my house to this day.
It is rusty around the edges and a little battered, and it
is also as holy a relic as I have ever seen.

Somebody said once, and a lot of us have been quoting it ever since, "Coincidences could be God's way of remaining anonymous." I have never been able to fit any notion of some kind of individual providence within the corners of my mind. You know what I mean by individual providence? That's the belief that ever and again God might look down on Tom Starnes and say, "You know, I think I'll take care of the old boy today. He's been a reasonably faithful sort." I've never been able, as one of my former bishops used to say, "get my head around that."

But I have come to believe that maybe Pascal was right: that the heart has its reasons that reason knows nothing about. And it just may be we are talking heart talk when we talk about the slender threads in our lives.

I can say "ours" can't I? You've had these slender threads, haven't you? Thought of any since I've been talking? I bet you give it some thought and you can remember some of those times when something or someone came your way, and touched you, just at a time it was most needed, and it changed your life.

A teacher of preaching was asked once how many points a sermon should have, and the professor said, "at least one."

The only point of this sermon is that our lives – yours and mine – are hidden in God's care, and, if we are sensitive to it, we can discern the slender threads that have made their appearances in our lives along the way. They have helped make us who we are, and we can depend on them coming our way as we move along with however much of life we have left.

Let me end with a prayer. The prayer was written by Theodore Parker Ferris, who, for years, was rector of Trinity Church in Boston. He wrote it on an American Airlines menu.

"Lord Jesus, I would like to be able to do myself the things I help others to do. I can give them a confidence I do not have. I can quiet their anxieties, but not my own. What do I lack? Or is it the way I am made? I want to be free to move from place to place without fear. And I want to face the things to be done without panic. You did it, and you made it possible for others to do it. . . . You trusted God. You didn't turn away from life. . . .You met each day as it came. I would like to do the same, but by myself I can't. I like to think that you can be with me, and in me, and that, with your help, I can do better. This is what I ask and hope for."

That's my prayer. Is it yours? I can't make it through life by myself. It's cute to say "life is a do it yourself project," and there is some truth to it, but certainly not the whole truth. The whole truth is that without God, and all those slender threads, we really can't do it ourselves. At least in the way we would like it to be done. So this prayer is my prayer, too.

Living between the Times

It was just about this time of year, some years back, when my wife and I sat down with a financial planner. No, these were not people to help you get out from under a mountain of debt; these were people who, hopefully, possessed the necessary skills to guide you into some profitable investment strategies.

We did not have much to invest. It had taken all we could muster to put three kids through college – without borrowing anything – and having two in at the same time for five years running. But, better late than never, we thought. The kids were finally on their own – at least we thought they were; no more braces on teeth or tuition payments, and, as a matter of fact, our kids were beginning to pick up the restaurant check ever and again. So, we had a little bit and we wanted to put it to the best use possible so that when we retired we could live in some "sun city" somewhere and have enough left over for plane fare to go sponge off the kids.

So we sat down with Rockville, Maryland's version of Sylvia Porter and talked about stocks versus bonds, and cash registers began jiggling in my head. That was a Tuesday, as I recall, and by Friday the financial skies had begun to turn grey and by Monday they were black. And I said, "Wouldn't you know it."

I said that because at that time that seemed to be the story of my life. Just as I would get to the store door the "open" sign would flip to "closed." When I would walk up to the ATM machine, it would either eat my card or tell me the system was down. I used to say that just about the time I would be ready to retire Social Security would go belly up.

So then it happened: Just when Wave and I sat down with a financial planner – considering cashing in on the market – the bottom drops out of the market.

Wave used to tell me that I made too much of this – and that I sounded a bit paranoid.

But it seemed to me that I had a pretty good case to make. When I was growing up in that Nazarene Church in Laurel – the one with the window I now have – there was a huge youth group; I couldn't wait to get old enough to join it. But when I did get old enough, my Dad decided he wanted to help revive a near-by church so we moved to a church that had no youth group.

Western Maryland College – now McDaniel College – a United Methodist School had, for years, given half tuition scholarships to children of ministers in the Baltimore Conference. They stopped that when I marched Tommy over to talk to them about financial aid.

The year I graduated from seminary, 1958, was the peak year in this country for worship attendance. It has been downhill all the way since then. I walk across the stage, get my diploma, ready to go to work and cash in on this bull church market, and the bottom drops out.

You see why I lived with my fear that the rug would always be pulled out from under me.

You know what brought this to mind – this day – Christ the King Sunday? It's called transition time in the church year. This is the last Sunday of the liturgical year. The season of Pentecost is ending and Advent is on its way: transition time.

Thanksgiving sort of fits into this time – a transition holiday – not religious, totally, just enough God to please those who care about such things, but not enough to make the football crazies or the gluttons feel guilty; and not enough God to keep us from having inter-faith worship services. There's nothing offensive about Thanksgiving – sort of a transitional holiday for transition time.

Now, the reason this made me think of all the ways life seems to have pulled the rug out from under me, is that in my better moments, when I wasn't thinking that somehow I had been singled out for preferential mistreatment, just maybe my life was being lived out in transition times.

There have been those times in history, you know, when the old order seems to be fading and the new is being ushered in. The Hebrew lesson today is from just such a time. The words you heard read today were David's last words. In such times it isn't all that clear what shape the new will take – "It doth not yet appear what we shall be" – or, put another way, "what will be." What is clear in these transition times is that the old is fading, and all we really know are the lines Bob Dylan taught us to sing, "The times, they are a changing."

Transition times – are we living in just such a time? It's hard to judge your own times. It's best to wait and let history be the judge.

But educated guesses don't hurt, and it looks like we are living in such times. Old orders are fading. Walls are tumbling down. Boundaries are being re-shaped; moral codes re-written and life-styles changing.

So let's just accept that it does seem to be the case that these are transition times. And what I would like to do today is think a bit about how we, as God's covenant people, are to live in these "in between" times.

And let me begin by suggesting that we accept this as fact. The times they are changing. Shifts are occurring; a lot is moving and shaking. This is just the way it is. We may wish it were not this way – that things would just stay the same – but that's not how life works.

> The moving finger writes, and having writ, moves on.

It's normal to long for a simpler time, a time when we all looked alike and thought alike; but that isn't the world in which we now live.

So we need to accept our own times, not sit longing for a time that is past and as the children of Israel learned to do as they sat in strange lands – lands so different from the ones they had known – they found ways to sing the Lord's songs even in those strange and distant lands. They had hung their harps up in the trees, the story says, because "how can you possibly sing the Lord's songs in strange and distant lands." Well, they made an amazing discovery; that's in this story, too. Zion's songs were meant for Babylon even; they were not limited to a certain time or a certain place. They could be sung anytime, anywhere – even in strange and distant lands.

So we, as God's people, need to accept our changing times as our days to live out our faith. Strange times, maybe, and not just changing but unsettling as well; however, Zion's songs were made to be sung anytime, anywhere, and if we don't sing them, who else will?

One other thing about transition times: Karl Barth, a famous German theologian of a few years back, said that we Christians are called to live "between the times." Whatever the times are like, the Christian is called to live as though they were transition times, because, in fact, they are.

Let me flesh this out a bit. It could be that we are living in transition times. But for those of us in here – those of us who call ourselves Christian – what else is new? If we are serious about our faith, serious about following in Jesus' steps, we will always be living between the times. We are a pilgrim people – in the world but not of the world. Our Biblical forbears ate unleavened bread. You know why? It was bread for those on the move; the same reason they lived in tents. This world was not their home; and it's not ours either. If we are serious about our faith, we are on a journey – "We're just a passing through."

So let's treasure the moment. This is our time to live; changing, chaotic, but full of promise also. Does no good to moan about it – long for a day long gone – and go around shouting "I want my country back." That's not the way life is. This is our time to live; God's gift to us.

Let me end with a Reinhold Niebuhr quote. He wrote:

> Nothing that is worth doing can be achieved in our lifetime; therefore we must be saved by hope. Nothing which is true or beautiful or good makes complete sense

in any immediate context of history; therefore we must
be saved by faith.

Niebuhr is letting us Christians know that we are living "between the times." "It doth not yet appear what we shall be." And given the way my mind works, a verse from a Fanny Crosby hymn I grew up singing came to mind.

> There are depths of love that I cannot know,
> Till I cross the narrow sea;
> There are heights of joy that I may not reach
> Till I rest in peace with thee.

In the meantime, . . .

Believing Without Seeing

During the Easter season the lectionary readings for the day do not include a Hebrew lesson. Instead, what are referred to as historical readings are included; these are usually from the Book of Acts.

Today's passage from Acts was, at first reading, my lesson of choice. This was start up time for what came to be called the Church of Jesus Christ. And what a group they saw themselves as being.

If this were occurring in our time we might call them communists; certainly we would call them socialists. Why? Well listen to how Luke describes them: not a one of them claimed private ownership of any possessions; everything they owned was held in common; "There was not a needy person among them, for as many as owned lands or houses sold them and brought the proceeds of what was sold," and laid them at the apostles' feet, "and it was distributed to each as any had need."

I so wanted to wade into this passage. In this day when we are crying "class warfare" because some are suggesting that those who have a lot maybe ought to give a bit more I felt we might need to remember that when we started out as a community of faith an article of that faith of ours was to see to it that the needy among us were taken care of.

But it was the gospel lesson that really hooked me; maybe because it concerns my namesake – Thomas – who was called the twin. Was he a Gemini, like me? Of two minds – on the one hand, but, then again, on the other hand: Thomas, the doubter. Well, the time in question in today's story is that he was indeed, the doubter.

It was evening on that first Easter Day. The disciples had gathered in some room somewhere, and security was tight. They were among the most wanted. The doors were locked and Jesus showed up. He tried to calm their fears and he had a gift for them: he breathed into them the power of the Holy Spirit.

But Thomas was absent. We aren't told why. He just missed the meeting, and when they told him what had happened, well, his good old Gemini gene kicked in and like any good Missourian said, "Show me." I need to see for myself, and that includes not just sight, but touch as well.

And Jesus made another visit. This time Thomas was there. And Jesus didn't seem all that upset with Thomas' initial doubt. Told him to go ahead and touch him, and when Thomas affirmed his faith, Jesus said to him: "Have you believed because you have seen? Well, blessed are those who have not seen and yet have come to believe."

That is to say, blessed are you and me because we have not seen, or touched, and yet we, most of us anyway, perhaps all of us here today, have come to believe. Oh, we have our questions – at least I hope we have – and we have our times of wondering – at least I hope we do – but it is fair to say that we believe. Why do we? And that's what I want to talk about. We believe without seeing. Why is that?

Know what popped into my head: the four principles that guided our founder, John Wesley, in his search for spiritual truth?

The first is the scriptures. This book that most of you carry around wrapped in that marvelously crafted cloth book jacket that Sue Collins made. What a treasure trove this collection of sacred writings. I certainly wouldn't believe as much as I do had I not been taught the wonderful stories that are found in these pages.

Know part of what I love about the window that Kenny Warrington tracked down for me – a window that just as I was hunt and pecking this out on my computer I cast a glance its way over to my left – is that it reminds me of some of those long dead saints in Laurel who taught me the stories of Jesus. When I was on my search at the Laurel Nazarene

Church I saw some of their names on the windows: Hazel Chambers, Mabel Adams, Wingate Tyndal.

Think of all the scribes – monks in solitude – who, over the centuries painstakingly copied from ancient manuscripts these sacred texts so that you and I might read.

I am one of these – and certainly not the only one – who believes that you just can't make this story up. Too many people, over too many centuries, writing in differing languages – agree on so many points. Of course there are differences in certain details. Eyewitnesses still don't always see eye to eye. But the basic truth is there. In the beginning, God created – and God continued to guide and direct – history is His story. As I said, you can't make this stuff up.

So, the Bible helps me to believe without seeing.

Wesley's second principle was reason – our God given ability to think and figure things out.

I know that the atheists among us are coming out of the closet. They don't call us believers stupid, but they seem to imply – sometimes even state – that we are engaging in a bit of delusional fancy.

Well, I have news for them. Some of the brightest, possessing the sharpest of minds, have found reason to believe. Bill Maher can hold our faith up to ridicule all he wants, but his reasoning against can't hold a candle to C. S. Lewis' reasoning for. To say this faith of ours is all gibberish is to fly in the face of that host of thinkers who, the deeper they dig into the nature of reality, are discovering, at the center of existence, not mere matter, but something more closely resembling spirit – a reality that is best described as mystery.

I had a bishop once who had an expression he used a lot. He would talk about trying to get his head around some issue. I may not be the brightest bulb in the chandelier, but I am a long way from being the dimmest. And for the life of me I can't get my head around the notion that we – all of us – just happened along; this marvelous creation of ours – nature following its courses, geese going along in formation, laws so dependable that we can land a man on the moon – just happening. Or that some obscure peasant couple could have a kid in some out of the way place, centuries ago, and that kid's name having taken its place high among all names.

I'm sorry. My reasoning tells me that you just can't make this stuff up.

Wesley's third point was tradition. I come back to my Warrington window. My brother tells me, and even though I think he re-writes our family history, that Daddy had that window put right next to our pew.

Can I tell you a story about that pew? It was really our pew. One Saturday morning my Dad went down to Small & Horsey hardware in Laurel and bought two hard rubber door stops. He then went by the church, unscrewed the second pew, shoved those door stops under the front of the pew, then screwed the pew back to the floor, and the Starnes family had the only reclining pew.

So that window I sat by as a kid, and now sit by as an old man, reminds me of those traditions that are so much a part of my life. And they are the source of my faith today: worship, hymns that just won't quit, rituals, like communion and baptisms, prayer meetings and testimonies.

And you have yours, and some that you are in the process of creating right now, that will sustain your faith in years to come.

I read about an Eskimo tribe in Canada that lived in the great tundra west of Hudson Bay. It seems that when these Eskimos would travel, they would stop along the way, and make a tower out of some rocks about the height of a man. They would then travel until they could no longer see the tower and then they would gather some more rocks and build another one. They would keep doing that all across the tundra – marking their route so that they would not lose their way.

My friend Mark Trotter from San Diego told that story in a sermon and he said that this is what a tradition is for – to prevent us from getting lost.

So I look at my window – Mr. & Mrs. Grady D. Starnes & family – and remember all those traditions – and I continue to believe even though I don't see.

Wesley's final principle was experience. And this really is the clincher for me.

I love the story that we have labeled, "The Man Born Blind." John tells it. The Pharisees were all bent out of shape because Jesus had healed him on the Sabbath. They then got into it with the man's parents questioning whether or not he had really been born blind. The parents tell the Pharisees to ask the kid. They do, and he utters those words I love: "Whether he is a sinner (meaning Jesus) or not, I do not know. What I do know is that once I was blind now I see."

Experience does it for me. You know my Dad's story. God's amazing grace touched him and changed our family's course. But I have a story too. There have been those times when I have, in my own way, been lost. And, at my wit's end, I have cried out for help, and help came.

And my children, all three of them, have a story to tell of God reaching down and guiding them through. They have all – each of them – had their times of needing some divine assistance and God has come through. .

And you do what I do for forty or so years and you see this powerful hand of God reaching down into people's lives – all kinds of people – and giving them strength for the living of their days. And I see it here.

No, I do not see. But I do believe, because my experience confirms my faith for me.

My son Tom, the lawyer, reads a lot, and sent me an Oxford Chapel sermon by Malcolm Muggeridge. Muggeridge was a journalist and philosopher who was converted and became a well-respected apologist for the faith. He's one of the brightest of minds that I was talking about previously. Let me end with this quote from that sermon:

> Words, just words! I can hear you saying. Well, yes, words; but there's something else – a man, who was born and lived like us; whose presence and teaching have continued to shine for generation after generation, just as they did for his disciples and for all who knew and listened to him in Galilee all those centuries ago. A man who died, but who none the less, in some quite unique way remained, and remains alive. A man who offered us the mysterious prospect of dying in order to live; who turned all the world's values upside down, telling us that it was the weak, not the strong, who mattered, the simple, not the learned, who understood, the poor, not the rich, who were blessed. A man whose cross, on which he died in agony, became the symbol of the wildest, sweetest hopes ever to be entertained.

Here's Muggeridge's last paragraph. But I'm going to plagiarize – steal his words and claim them as my own way to wind this sermon up.

> And now? Well, all I can say is, as one aging and singularly unimportant fellow-man, that I have conscientiously looked far and wide, inside and outside my own head and heart, and I have found nothing other than this man and his words which offers any answer to the dilemmas of this tragic, troubled time.

God's Foolishness
is Our Wisdom

I had every intention of using the gospel lessons as the bases for my Lenten sermons, and use one of the other three gospel lessons for our Wednesday night Bible studies. So today my intention was to deal with John's telling of the time Jesus plaited a whip of cords and chased the money changers, along with their animals, out of the temple.

But when I read the other lessons I decided to change my mind. We preachers never know for sure about these things, even though some of us claim to know for sure, but I would like to think that it was God who nudged me – shoved me, really – in the direction of the Ten Commandments.

I might not have been persuaded to change my sermonic mind had it not been for the words Paul wrote in one of his letters to the church at Corinth – words about God's foolishness, or God's perceived foolishness, being wiser than the world's supposed wisdom.

Back in 1959, when I "cast my lot with the people called Methodists" and opened the Book of Worship to the communion ritual, I noticed that a reading of the Ten Commandments was a part of the ritual. I never knew why it got removed, along with the required reading of the Beatitudes. But it did.

It's probably a safe bet to make that the Ten Commandments also got removed from most preachers' lists of suggested sermon topics. It surely did from mine. When I was looking through old sermons to cull out any

I might not want to throw in the recycling bin, I found a Lenten sermon series I did on the Ten Commandments back in the early sixties. To my best recollection I have never preached a whole sermon on them since.

They were in the news a few years back when a court somewhere in the south wanted to have the Ten Commandments posted in its courtroom. I don't remember how that ended. But other than that, they aren't in the news much.

Nor are they anywhere, much. At least that's the way it seems to me. I doubt if we teach them to our children – at home I mean. I guess they come up occasionally in Sunday Schools and, I would guess, in most synagogues.

But what's it to me, and why did I decide to preach about them today, forgetting all about Jesus chasing money changers out of the temple?

I'm not sure really. It could be – and you don't know how much it pains me to admit this – the whole Rush Limbaugh incident. Let me hasten to say – and I can't hasten fast enough to say – that Rush is not the only one who has gone potty mouth on us in public. There have been a few from the left side of the political spectrum who have done it. But since he seems to be the most recent he gets the credit for reminding me of something that I have long since felt is occurring: the coarsening of our culture. Words that used to never be uttered in public, now get said – sometimes shouted – by respectable people, no less.

When Rachel, our first grandchild, hit her teen years, her tastes in music veered sharply away from her granddad's tastes. She would get in the car with me and immediately hit the scan button, leaving my public radio station behind. So, we are tootleing along one afternoon; I'm not paying any attention to the noise she is listening to, until I hear a word that sounds a lot like one of the those words that really should not be spoken in public. "Rachel, that's awful. You shouldn't be listening to such things." "Oh, Pop Pop."

A coarsening of the culture. Obscene words, degrading words, being given wide audiences and when set to music receiving Grammy awards for artistic achievement.

Something else turned my head toward Moses and Mt. Sinai. I know none of the commandments say, specifically, thou shalt not lie, but we have interpreted the 9th one about "bearing false witness" to mean that. And any ethical code drawn up has stated that lying is a no-no.

Well, lying, like daffodils, are now in full bloom. Billions of dollars are being spent to spread lies, and in this sense specifically break the 9th commandment, by bearing false witness against the one you are trying to beat in the primary.

Whatever turned my head in the direction of the Commandments is beside the point, really. What is the point is why I think we need to re-visit them occasionally.

For one thing, it would help us to remember how they came to be. Most of us know the story. God was in the process of fashioning a community of believers. These were to be His covenant community. And what a covenant community needs is a covenant. So Moses goes up to the top of Mt. Sinai and our faith history reads that God gave Moses the laws that were to govern his chosen people.

Communities need rules to live by – especially newly forming communities. When the kids were young we went to Jamestown, Virginia. The guide was telling us about some of the rules that were established to govern that brand new colony. One had to do with church attendance, which was mandatory: miss once and you get flogged; miss twice and you get thrown in jail; miss three times and you get shot. I thought that a bit harsh, and I expressed my opinion to the guide. Know how he answered me: he said that in a new community, it is important that there be community discipline. All our lives depend on mutual obedience to the rules we have adopted as a community.

So God says, through Moses, we are in this together. There can be only one God; no idols to other gods. Don't take my name in vain – don't treat it lightly or profane it. Set aside one day and make it holy. Honor your parents — respect them. Don't, under any circumstances, kill anybody. Life is sacred. And don't mess around with someone else's husband or wife. Marriage covenants are holy and binding. Don't take anything that doesn't belong to you — it's not yours; work for your own stuff. And let your yes be yes and your no, no. Don't make a false witness. And be satisfied with what you have. Don't be always looking over to the other side of the fence where the grass always looks a whole lot greener than it looks on your side of the fence.

Which brings me to Paul's words in his letter to the Church at Corinth: "You think you're so smart — all your worldly wisdom. You are convinced that all I have been preaching to you is just so much foolishness. But, let me tell you something, folks; in my book, God's wisdom has made foolish the wisdom of the world, and, furthermore, God's foolishness is wiser than human wisdom."

I'm reasonably sure a fair number of us don't believe Paul. These are different times, we say. Ours is a new day. Those ancient rules don't apply anymore — well maybe some of them need to be kept, but even those may need to be modified a bit. Didn't Bob Dylan remind us that the "Times, they are a changing."

There's an old story I love. A farmer had a rooster who lived in a coop at the bend of a railroad track. Every evening when the night train would come through, and its headlight would shine into that chicken coop, the old rooster would run outside and crow because he thought it was the dawn of a new day. The seminary professor who told that story then said that he had lived through the dawn of a lot of new days.

Truth is each generation thinks its times are different and, in some ways, unique. But do we ever outgrow our need to pay attention to God's rules? There is an ancient Chinese proverb that says: "He who spits at heaven spits in his own face."

Robert Bellah, an influential ethicist in our day says that our problem as a society is that we seem to have lost the ability to, as he puts it, "language the common good." All that this means is that we as a society seem to have lost our sense of what is right and what is wrong – what is appropriate behavior.

We spiritual descendants of Moses and the covenant people ought to be ready with a suggestion: what about this old code of conduct – these Ten Commandments? It seems to me to be a pretty good basis for, as Bellah put it, "languaging the common good."

Let me end with a story out of the life of Albert Schweitzer. Most of us know how he spent his life as a doctor in South Africa, where he lived out his philosophy of "reverence for life."

He tells that he was seven or eight years old when he and a young friend made themselves a couple catapults – what we would call slingshots. They were going to blast away at some birds. He really didn't want to do it – he loved the birds' singing and besides that, his reverence for all of life was already taking shape in his mind and heart. But he didn't want to be laughed at, or called a sissy, so he went along. He and his friend crouched behind some bushes, and just as they were getting ready to fire away, the church bells began to ring,

> Mingling their music with the songs of the birds and the sunshine. It was the Warning-bell, which began half an hour before the regular peal-ringing, and for me it was a voice from heaven. I shooed the birds away, so that they flew where they were safe from my companion's catapult, and then I fled home. And ever since then, when the Passiontide bells ring out to the leafless trees and the sunshine, I reflect with a rush of grateful emotion how on that day their music drove deep into my heart the commandment: "Thou shalt not kill."

Maybe you and I can't change society – make it any more ready to obey God's commandments. What we can do – you and I – is allow the reminders of God in our lives – whatever those bells might happen to be – calling us to remember who we are – God's children, who choose not only to trust, but also to obey.

Philip and the Ethiopian Eunuch

During the Easter season there are no Hebrew lessons listed in the lectionary. In their place are listed what are referred to as "Historic" messages; all from the Book of Acts.

An historic message – that intrigued me. "Marching orders" for the church came to mind. I thought of "framers" as in the writers of the Constitution, and "original intent" as in what our founding fathers in the faith really had in mind for this gathering of believers that was in the making – the Church – the body of Christ.

Historic Message: On Easter Day we had Peter preaching that God shows no partiality: ".in every nation anyone who fears him and does what is right is acceptable to him." And then he told of how God sent Jesus – the eternal word – and how this gift from God went about doing good – healing all the oppressed – and how he was killed and God raised him and we are to be his witnesses. The historic message: the church is to preach the risen Christ to everyone.

In the second Sunday of Easter, the historic message was those words from Acts that make us capitalists sit up and take notice: nothing we have is ours alone. It is ours to share with those who are in need. The Historic message: what we have is really not ours, but God's; it has merely been entrusted to our care.

The historic message for the third Sunday was that the church is to be a healing station. And the fourth Sunday showed Peter standing toe to toe with the supreme high command telling them who really was in control of things. The historic message: the church is to be prophetic; to say and say clearly, "thus says the Lord."

And now today – the fifth Sunday of Easter – the historic message is a story.

Philip, one of the twelve Christ picked out to get this whole thing started, was traveling south along the Gaza strip – on foot, because the scriptures say that he had to run to catch up with a chariot that had passed him by. Now the reason Philip wanted to catch this Ben Hur type is because the Spirit moved him to do so. At least that's what Luke says moved him.

It could have been. However, it could also have been the sight of a well-healed eunuch, "a minister of the Queen of Ethiopia," riding along reading from the prophet Isaiah. (Don't ask me how Philip knew it was Isaiah he was reading. I didn't write the story.)

Anyway, Philip ran on ahead and caught up with this Ethiopian, and interpreted Isaiah to him, helped him hear the good news, baptized him in the river and the eunuch went on his way rejoicing.

That's the story. The historic message – well, it all depends.

When I was first told this story in Sunday school (did I raise my hand and ask Virgil Foskey, or Gertrude Mitchell, or Mabel Adams, "what's a eunuch?") I'm sure I didn't, simply because the eunuch's sexuality was not the point of this story as I was taught it. The point was one of personal evangelism. Philip was a faithful Christian and he collared this guy riding by and gave testimony to him, and the eunuch got saved, as we say, and Philip had been faithful to do his duty, now you go and do likewise.

That's the historic message I first heard in this story.

It's also the historic message I read when I was given a brand new set of the Interpreter's Bible – a moderate to liberal collection of commentaries, in the late 50's – hot off the Abingdon Press. Philip was being a faithful witness is what the Reverend Doctor Theodore Parker Ferris, a noted "Prince of the Pulpit", who wrote the exposition for the Book of Acts in the Interpreter's Bible, said is the "historic message" of this story.

It isn't. And I doubt seriously if Dr. Ferris were writing today, he would say so. Personal witnessing may be <u>a</u> point of this story, but it's hard to make the case that it is <u>the</u> point. And the reason I say this is that there are two other stories that Luke tells in this 8th chapter of Acts – stories which, I think, carry the same "historic message" to the church.

The first story tells about the time Philip went into Samaria to preach Christ crucified and risen and to heal the sick. The second story concerns a man named Simon, a magician, whom Philip baptized and took along to help him in his work. And, of course, the third story is about Philip's encounter with the Ethiopian eunuch.

These are the stories in this 8th chapter of Acts and all, to be sure, have something to say about Philip's faithfulness as a personal evangelist. But, I contend, that is not the "historic message."

The "historic message?" Remember the one for Easter Day – Peter's sermon – in which he said that God showed no partiality. Anyone, Peter preached, regardless of sex, race, national origin can come in. Ho! Everyone who thirsts, come on down and drink deeply of the water of life. Just as you are – without one plea. That's the historic message. As Robert Frost put it in his poem, "The Mending Wall," "something there is that doesn't love a wall," the same can be said for God. There are to be no walls, and Jesus went around tearing down all walls that divide. And his church – to be the church – must always have an open door policy.

That's what these three stories are saying – isn't it? Samaritans – goodness gracious – a mixed breed; racially impure, therefore, racially inferior. They certainly could not be a part of any kingdom that was to come. Jesus had chipped away at this notion – talking to a Samaritan woman, no less, in a public place, and making a Samaritan the hero in one of his most significant stories. And now, would you believe it, Philip goes down into a Samaritan village and says, "You all come, you hear."

And magicians – horrors! Sorcery, witchcraft – all of a piece – the work of demons. Steer clear of all this, whatever you do. But good old Philip makes friends with Simon, the Magnificent, and brings him into the fold.

And if all that isn't enough, Philip cozies up to a sexual deviant and baptizes him into the faith, when everyone knows, for God's sake, that anything less than a full-blooded, raw-boned he-man is something less than human, and can't, absolutely can't, be accepted into God's kingdom on anything like equal terms.

Oh, yes they can, our historic messages say. Over and over again they say it – God shows no partiality and neither must you. The doors of this church that is being built, whose foundation we are now laying, can have no other foundation than this – Jesus Christ – and he said that any house being built, using him as a foundation, would have no restrictive clauses in its deed; its doors would always be open to anybody. This, I think, is the historic message from this story.

It is noteworthy that this lesson falls on the day that the General Conference of the United Methodist Church is winding up its business in Tampa, Florida. And a major item it has had on its agenda this year is the same one it has had on its agenda since the early seventies: how open and accepting will our church be to those who are sexually different. Some think it is shameful that this issue should still dominate our denomination's official proceedings.

I do not think it shameful. It has to be, simply because this is a struggle for the soul of our church. Sexual issues are not easy for the church – never have been. There are questions and deep seated fears. I know.

But the church isn't comfortable shutting people out. You see, enough of us have gotten the point along the way – the point of the stories in the 8th chapter of Acts – that God shows no partiality and neither should we. Just because someone's race is different – as were the Samaritans – or we call someone a witch or a sorcerer – as was Simon and his followers – or someone was sexually different – as the eunuch – just because they are different does not disqualify them. At some level, we, the church, have heard this – have gotten the point – and so we have struggled.

We Methodists struggled over a hundred years ago with the race question, and the historic message of the church lost out and we built walls that divided us. This is why you have two Methodist churches in so many of these eastern shore towns: at one time each was a different denomination – one northern and one southern – a result of a split over the issue of slavery. We are still trying to bind up those wounds.

And now, we Methodists are still struggling – those who want to say no to those, who, in their eyes do not measure up – sexually or otherwise – and those who say, "Hold on now, God shows no partiality, can we?"

Can I end with a gospel word – where even historic messages ought to end? It's from good old John's pen. He had lived a long life; had seen about all there was to see. Tradition has it that he was blind. He had walked closely with Jesus. He was summing it all up when he said:

> Beloved, let us love one another; for love is of God, and he who loves is born of God and knows God. He who does not love does not know God; for God is love. . . .There is no fear in love, but perfect love casts out fear. . . .If anyone says, 'I love God,' and hates his brother, he is a liar; for he who does not love his brother whom he has seen, cannot love God whom he has not seen. And this is the commandment we have from him, that he who loves God should love his brother also.

A God who is love sends a son to live love. Jesus lived love, and those who walked with him were taught to love. They were also taught that this love was the greatest – even greater than faith and hope. And the love Jesus lived and taught opened doors; it did not close them. And the church this love built must also be a church – always – of the open door.

Handling Life's Second Bests

I altered the scripture lesson a bit. As soon as I started to read it, I knew I wanted to back up.

Today's assigned reading was about Paul's vision – there go those dreams again – about a man from Macedonia pleading for Paul to come there and give them some help. Paul went. But that's not where he had intended to go – not even the way he had wanted to go. So I backed up in the story to the part that was read to you today.

Paul had wanted to preach the gospel in Asia Minor – the place known as Turkey today. He specifically wanted to go to the region of Bythnia – a rich, fertile, bustling area with a number of prospering Greek-speaking cities. Fertile ground for spreading the gospel. But for some reason, as the writer of Acts puts it, "the spirit of Jesus" blocked their passage; they went down to Troas, where Paul had his vision about coming over into Macedonia, and the rest is early church history.

Changed plans, hopes dashed, having to take second best, has that ever happened to you?

When I was in seminary, we were told – actually required – to read the sermons of the great preachers. We were told that poets read other poets – a sermon is a particular art form, or should be – so you boys (which is what we were then) need to read these old guys.

One of my favorites was Harry Emerson Fosdick. He was pastor of Riverside Church in New York City, and one of his sermons that I read was titled "Handling Life's Second Bests." Yes, I stole his title. His text for that sermon is the passage we read today about Paul having to go with an option – a second choice – second best.

Fosdick cites some famous cases: Whistler, a noted American painter that most of us know because of the painting he did of his mother. Well, as Fosdick tells the story Whistler hadn't started out to be a painter; he really wanted to be a soldier, but he flunked out of West Point because he flunked chemistry, causing him to quip, "If silicon had been a gas, I should have become a major general." Phillips Brooks, famed preacher at Trinity Church in Boston, who wrote the Christmas carol we all love – I think it is the best one – "O Little Town of Bethlehem," wanted to be a teacher but he failed miserably in the classroom, and turned to preaching as a default position.

Fosdick lists others: Sir Walter Scott wanted to be a poet, but he was bad at it, so he settled on writing adventure novels that we are still reading. Lupus caused Flannery O' Connor to move back home in the south to live with her mother and it was there in her second best place that she wrote so movingly.

Let me bring this closer to home. In 1967 I got a call from the President of Wesley College, Dr. Robert Parker asking me if I would come to Wesley as chaplain. Dr. Parker was from the Baltimore Conference so I knew him. I said that yes, I would.

What really attracted me was that I could come home, to Delaware, be near my family, and also be on a college campus. I was really excited and absolutely convinced that this was what God had in mind for my life.

Luckily we didn't go get any packing boxes, because Dr. Parker called me and said that the Bishop and his cabinet in the Peninsula Conference informed him know that that position belonged to this conference. So they sent one of their own, Ed Wilkins, a Millsboro boy, and I was left hanging.

But not for long, and like Paul, I couldn't go to my Bythnia, but I did go to Bowie – a new town, a new church, a glorious place to raise a family, very near the University of Maryland where Wave could pursue her graduate studies; I could help build a sanctuary. This summer will go there to join a lot of those folks I took into membership and together we will celebrate 50 glorious years of service to that community.

Which brings me to my first point: we just never know what God has in mind for us. There is a poem whose authorship is in question. Some say it was written by an unknown Confederate soldier.

> I asked God for strength, that I might achieve,
> I was made weak that I might learn humbly to obey.
> I asked for health that I might do greater things,
> I was given infirmity that I might do better things.
> I asked for riches that I might be happy,
> I was given poverty that I might be wise.
> I asked for power that I might have the praise of others,
> I was given weakness that I might feel the need of God.
> I asked for all things that I might enjoy life.
> I was given life that I might enjoy all things.
> I got nothing that I asked for, but everything I had hoped for,
> Almost despite myself, my prayers were answered.
> I am, among all people, most richly blessed.

Have any stories from your own life come to mind – careers you had planned to pursue; jobs that you thought you had lined up; dreams for yourself or even for your children; and you had to accept a second best? Maybe God had other things in mind for you; maybe even better things.

A teacher in a rabbinic school said, "I counsel my students on the eve of their graduation from rabbinic school, all terrified that they won't get the job they want: 'Relax, because God is going to put you where God wants you – whether you like it or not.'"

I have a friend from my college days – he calls himself a spiritual pagan; his growing up in the Nazarene Church soured him on organized religion. However, he prays and trusts God, and when he gets on the phone with me from Maine, we will break into singing some of those wonderful Red Book songs that we both cut our spiritual eye teeth on. But Gerry will say to me if, in one of our conversations, I start to question what I am doing, "Brother Tom, you are where God wants you to be."

When some of the folks at Epworth Church see me, the point they invariably make about our daughter, Vicky – their pastor – is that "she seems so at ease, so comfortable in her own skin." I tell them that that's because she believes she is where God wants her to be.

Which leads me to the other point of this sermon: Paul couldn't go to Asia Minor. God had other plans. So he accepted his second best as the best and decided to, as we say, "bloom where he was planted," which is what we are called to do: bloom where we are planted.

There are some wonderful lines in the book of Jeremiah. Jeremiah is writing to the children of Israel who are exiled in Babylon. Talk about second bests. This was certainly not the way these chosen of God wanted their lives to end up. But Jeremiah told them that God's word to them was quite simple: bloom where you are planted. Build some houses; raise families; plant gardens and eat the produce; marry off your children. "Seek the welfare of the city where I have sent you into exile, and pray to the Lord on its behalf, for in its welfare you will find your welfare." This is where you have ended up, God says, so live with it, and make the most of it.

I have another rabbi story for you. I love rabbi stories. This story is about a man who left his house to find a treasure. He wanted to find the meaning of life, something that he couldn't find in the hum-drum existence of his own life. So he took to the road in search of this treasure that he knew was out there somewhere.

The first night he slept out under the stars. He took his shoes off and put them down beside the blanket he was sleeping on, pointed in the direction of the way he had been walking. While he slept a prankster came along and turned the man's shoes in the opposite direction, so that when he put his shoes on the next morning, instead of walking in the direction he had been walking, he started walking back in the direction from which he had come.

He travelled some distance and then noticed a house that looked strangely familiar. He went inside the house and was greeted by a family that looked remarkably like his family. So he settled in there and discovered the treasure that he was looking for.

Hardly any of our lives go as we planned. For some of us there have been detours along the way. For others of us it has been a matter of scaling back hopes and dreams and settling for new realities, and, like Paul, heading down a different path than the one we might have wished to head down.

So, my message today is, quite simply, my friend Gerry's word to me: you are where God wants you to be. And, wherever we are, God's will for us is that we make the most of it, doing as Jeremiah instructed, bloom where we are planted.

Made for More than This

Winston Churchill said once that there was nothing more exhilarating than to be shot at and missed. I thought of that as Wave and I awakened in our hotel room in Boston Monday morning having weathered the storm, Sandy.

Thought of it more when we heard that grandson Jacob, whom we had just seen a couple days before in Philadelphia, had also weathered the storm and was safely situated in his apartment, with enough food and supplies. Thought of it even more when we heard that grandson Dylan, whom we had spent Friday with in the borough of Queens in New York, was also safe and sound. Queens, as you have probably heard, got hit broadside.

My exhilaration over the ones I loved getting spared left me pretty quickly when I kept watching the news and saw all those helpless people who took the shot that had missed me and my loved ones.

It was about this time that the card catalogue in my head called to mind another quote. Had to wait to get home and check that notebook where I have all these snippets of information stored away.

It's a quote by Harry Golden. Harry Golden was a journalist for the Charlotte, North Carolina Observer newspaper. He also published a newsletter which he titled, "The Carolina Israelite." He once offered a solution to the problem of school integration in the south: he said just take out the seats; let the kids stand up at their desks. People don't seem to mind standing up with blacks; they just don't want to sit down with them.

But that isn't the quote I thought of as I watched CNN and the Weather Channel. I thought of the one when he wrote a column about the origins of the universe: how over a period of millions of years the planet earth came to be, and water came about, and plants and animals and human beings – and while thinking about the mystery and grandeur of all that – here's how he said it: "Contemplating this, it helped put in perspective the news that my flight from Charlotte to New York had just been cancelled."

Now I wouldn't want to swear to it, but I think this quote came to mind as a reporter, with voice choking, told about seeing neighbors in Queens, who had lost everything – everything – run into one of their neighbors and ask if there was anything they could do for them. Then, together, gave thanks that they had been spared.

Houses gone; cars gone; clothes gone; all those things that we value so highly, and even go so deeply in debt to get, really don't matter all that much. Sandy caused all of us to snap to attention and remember what really gives meaning to life.

There is such a thing as pulpit license. What this means is that preachers can make leaps – giant leaps, sometimes – to make a point. We preachers have been known to stretch scripture passages to try and get them to say what we had in mind to say anyway.

I hope I am not stretching it too much to say that All Saints Sunday is a time for us to come to attention and remember what really gives meaning to life, and, in this case, remember those who have given meaning to our lives.

Now the church that I cut my faith eye teeth on had no such Sunday. When it came to Saints, that was all a part of that Catholic idol worship talk, and we wanted nothing to do with it. None of our Nazarene churches were named for saints. Ours were numbered, and come to think of it, I never remember any 2nd Churches of the Nazarene; ours were always First churches, or named after a street or a town.

It is true that All Saints Day began to hallow the memories of the canonized Saints, but the day was kept after the Reformation and Protestants have continued to set aside the day to commemorate all those who, as we say, "have died in the Lord."

"For all the saints, who from their labors rest" are words we just sang. There are saints I remember.

Last Sunday morning Wave and I took granddaughter Rachel, senior at Boston University, out to Eastern Nazarene College. We walked over to the entrance of Munro Hall – girls' dormitory – and showed her the spot outside the main entrance where Wave and I would linger, holding hands, until the curfew called an ending to the day.

Dean Munro. What a saint. A Radcliffe graduate, who instilled in Wave and me a love of literature that lasts to this day; she wrote devotional books that are still around, and her example of living the sanctified life gave me the most pause in contemplating my leaving the Nazarene church.

We walked past Mann Student center named after President Mann. What a stalwart; what a saint in my life. We went into the administration building where most of our classes were held and the procession of saints marched across the stages in Wave's and my head: Tim Smith, Wilbur Mullen, Charlie Akers, Louise Dygoski, and Prof. Span. For all the Saints. And you have yours to recall. Oh, how rich our lives are because of all these saints who now rest from their labors.

Something else All Saints Sunday can do for us. Not just let us know what is really important in life, but also to remind us that this life is not all there is.

On August 31, 1776, Benjamin Franklin wrote out his epitaph.

>The Body of
>B. Franklin, Printer,
>Like the cover of an old book,
>Its contents torn out,

> And stripped of its Lettering and Gilding,
> Lies here, Food for Worms.
> But the Work shall not be lost,
> For it will, as he believ'd, appear once more
> In a new and more elegant Edition
> Corrected and improved
> By the Author.

Which calls to mind another snippet rumbling around in my head – didn't want to look it up – but someone, sometime said, if this life is all there is, then we are over-provided for. All that means is that each one of us is made for more than this – and at some level we all sense it.

I have so many favorites of things that I hesitate to say that Thornton Wilder's play, Our Town, is my favorite. I have seen it so many times. Son Tommy was in it at the church he attended in Washington. His son, Joe, played Dr. Gibbs in his high school version. I saw it in an off-Broadway theater a couple years ago. Here's the part I love best. Those of you who know the play know that the central character is a voice – the stage manager – and he speaks this part:

> We all know that something is eternal. And it ain't houses and it ain't names, and it ain't earth, and it ain't even the stars. . .everybody knows in their bones that something is eternal, and that something has to do with human beings. All the greatest people ever lived have been telling us that for five thousand years and yet you'd be surprised how people are always losing hold of it. There's something way down deep that's eternal about every human being.

We do lose hold of it as Wilder suggests, until a storm comes and washes away all that we thought was important, and we come upon a Sunday to remind us of all the saints who have blessed our lives and to remind us, also, that this world really is not our home; we're just a passing through.

The Faith of Job

The Job story is a favorite of mine, and, I would guess, seeing as how this ancient tale has been told and re-told in various art forms over the years, a favorite of many.

But, I have always wished for a different ending to the story – at least in my later years. Oh, don't get me wrong, I do love happy endings – "and they all lived happily ever after" – still wish for them after all these years. I would have thought, though, that the writer of the book of Job – dealing realistically as he or she did with this age-old problem of evil – could have been a bit more realistic with the ending.

Like ending the story with the lesson for today. You see that's where most of the life stories I know anything about usually end up: scores not being settled; lost fortunes not being recouped – never mind getting doubled. I grew up on a theology of faith as success. A song I learned early on was "Only believe, only believe, all things are possible, only believe." And every time a travelling evangelist came to our little church in southern Delaware, Daddy would bring him out to our house to anoint my brother Benton and pray for his healing. But the muscular dystrophy never went away, and we were left feeling that our lack of faith was keeping Benton from being able to walk.

It's still around, this notion of faith as happy ending. My wife and I were back visiting in a church I had recently served. During the sharing of joys and concerns, we were told that a woman for whom the church had been praying for had been healed of her cancer. Everyone applauded; praise God for this triumph of faith. Sitting in the congregation, listening to this healing success story, was a mother and daughter, who, just a short month ago, sat in that same sanctuary as we celebrated the life of her husband, who, after months and months of praying, by that same congregation, died. The "effectual, fervent prayers" of Epworth Church for Jim just didn't do the trick for him.

So I wish the Job story had a different ending and I will give it one this time around by winding it up with the lesson for today – these wonderful lines:

I had heard of you by the hearing of the ear,

But now my eyes see you.

There's a line in the book of James, "you have heard of the patience of Job." Today, I want us to try and hear of the faith of Job; let me suggest a few of its characteristics.

The first is so obvious: his faith was his. Rumbling around in his head were all those notions of God he had been taught. He had heard much about the "Holy One." Plenty of people had told him plenty. He had heard it all.

And they kept at it: believe this; believe that. God is like this; God is like that. Job had heard all this, but now he saw. His eyes were opened. It was his faith; his alone.

Which is probably why the Gospel lesson chosen for this Sunday is the story of Blind Bartimaeus, a beggar, sitting by the roadside, whose only request was to be able to see again – a request that was granted.

Faith as sight: "I've heard it all. Oh, please let me see for myself." Not faith as success, "and they all lived happily ever after," but faith as sight. This was the faith of Job.

The second marker of Job's faith is that it was born of struggle. There were the doubts and the questions: "Let the day perish in which I was born....Why did I not die at birth?" "I will say to God, do not condemn me; let me know why you contend against me." "For there is hope for a tree, if it is cut down."

A Buddhist adage says, "If you walk only on sunny days, you will never reach your destination." Gene Mauch managed in baseball's major leagues for quite a few years, and piled up an impressive number of winning seasons. But none of his teams ever reached the World Series. He suffered more than his share of personal tragedy. He said once: "If it's true that you learn from adversity, then I must be the smartest SOB in the world."

I have come to believe that it is true that adversity can teach us a few things. I have further come to believe that faith, at least a faith that approaches the real thing – and is truly our own – can only come after struggle. Remember Stephan Crane's poem, "The Wayfarer?"

> A wayfarer, perceiving the pathway of truth was astonished.
>
> It was thickly grown up with weeds.
>
> 'Aha,' he said. 'I perceive that no one has passed this way in a long time.'
>
> Then he saw that each blade was a singular knife.
>
> 'Well,' he muttered, 'doubtless there are other ways.'

I am not sure there are other ways, other than the way of struggle, to a life of faith – a faith that opens our soul's eyes. One of my favorite preachers was John Vanoorsdal who, in addition to serving as chaplain at Yale University, was, for a number of years, the preacher on the radio program, The Protestant Hour. He wrote:

> It is important to understand the students who now fill the classrooms of our seminaries, . . . Increasing numbers are not at all the young, glad-eyed, wholesome, and unsullied youth we imagine from former times. They may never have been what we imagined. But now there

is no pretense as increasing numbers come divorced, recovering alcoholics, social workers still wearing the halo of sadness earned on city streets, nurses and medical technicians sober eyed from the emergency rooms of hospitals. These, increasing numbers of them, are Good Friday's seminarians who have heard the ancient witness of Elijah and the widow's son, of Jesus and the widow's son, and Paul on the road to Damascus, but who know from their own experience that God in our time is known in the restorations, the healings, the reversals which occur in all the old familiar places.

All of this echoing the words of a hymn I learned to sing as a child,

> I must needs go home by the way of the cross,
> There's no other way than this.

For my money, the faith of Job – the kind of faith that sees – really sees – only comes out of soul struggles.

Integrity was a part of Job's faith. He kept his own counsel. He didn't let his friends turn his head.

God knows they tried. Zophar certainly did: "Know then that God exacts of you less than your guilt deserves." And Eliphaz, thinking he had a corner on the truth, threw this verbal jab at Job: "Think now, who that was innocent ever perished?"

Job would have none of it. He held on to his integrity. "I have heard many such things; miserable comforters are you all. Have windy words no limit?" Reminiscent of Bertrand Russell's comment: "The trouble with the world is that the stupid are cocksure and the intelligent are full of doubt." No, there was only one way for Job. He had to maintain his integrity. He would not admit something that he did not feel was true. He would, as he put it, continue to speak to the almighty and argue (his) case with God. Integrity was a part of the faith of Job.

Trust was also. "Though he slay me, yet will I trust him." Don't get caught up in the fruitless argument, I think, of whether or not God causes evil. Elie Wiesel says that all the great questions remain unanswered, and this is one of the greatest questions. The point here is Job's trust, and the price for it was letting God be in charge.

I love that great deposition by God. "Where were you, Job, when I laid the foundations of the earth?" "Have you commanded the morning since your days began and caused the dawn to know its place?" "Do you give the horse its might?" Huh? Do you? "Is it by your wisdom that the hawk soars, and spreads its wings toward the south?" Job had to know his place. He wasn't God. There is a story told about the time Queen Victoria was in her royal yacht on the Irish Sea. That sea is known to be particularly impetuous and a sudden storm came up causing the ship to bounce up and down as though it were a toy boat. When they finally made it to port, the Queen said to her doctor who had accompanied her, "Go up at once, Sir James, and give the admiral my compliments and tell him the thing must not occur again."

Job's faith was a matter of resting in the Lord. It was "turning it over" as more than just a few of us now say, knowing that we aren't God and we need help. It is such an old saw I am embarrassed to repeat it, but I will anyway: if God is our co-pilot, then we are sitting in the wrong seat.

So much of my faith is wrapped up in the hymns I grew up singing. Let me end with this one:

> God hath not promised skies always blue,
> Flower strewn pathways, all our lives through.
> God hath not promised sun without rain,
> Joy without sorrow, peace without pain;
> But God hath promised strength for the day,
> Rest for the labor, light for the way;
> Grace for the trials, help from above;
> Unfailing kindness, undying love.

And that, my friends, is the faith of Job.

All I Have Needed

The Elijah story from last week – about his encounter with the prophets of Baal – is **a** rather widely known one from this major prophet's life. Not so the story today, I would guess; except to me. And I remember it well.

Actually, I remember the first time I heard it. It had not been a favorite for the preachers I listened to as a kid. It didn't have enough judgment in it I suppose.

It was just about this time of year and I was fulfilling a long standing dream: I was singing in a male quartet, starting out on a summer of touring for my college – a small church college up in the suburbs of Boston struggling to build buildings and find students. So the college sent four of us groups out to take building pledges and enroll some students. A college representative travelled with us.

One night Ken Pearsall, vice-president for development – his actual title was "field representative" – stood to preach and told this story about Elijah and the widow woman who gave up her last bit of oil and meal – subjecting her and her son to starvation – to the prophet. And tall, handsome, Ken Pearsall – who became a mentor of mine – baptized both Vicky and Tommy – felt some disappointment when I bolted the Nazarene Church and became a Methodist – lost touch for twenty plus years – bumped into each other at a college homecoming – and he looked at this now 60 year old – stared a bit, and said, "It's the eyes; I remember the eyes" – took this story – especially the lines, "For thus says the Lord God of Israel: the jar of meal will not be emptied and the jug of oil will not fail until the Lord sends rain on the earth." He took that line and told those people that God could take their little bit and bless it – use it to help educate young people in a Christian college; and not only that, he said that God would not let Eastern Nazarene College fail – God would provide.

But the story stamped itself on my soul for reasons other than my admiration and respect for Ken Pearsall. Its message of God's coming through – his great faithfulness – hit home with me at a very troubling time in my life.

My first year in college had not been easy. I graduated first among the boys in the class of 1950 at Laurel High School. The few girls that beat me out had not taken all the math and science courses I had taken. They had taken typing and home economics.

Even taking the academic course as I had, I breezed through high school. College was different. The reading assignments – I had never seen such requirements. And term papers – I had never written one. So I was swamped and had just received a letter from the college saying that I was on academic probation.

Then there was the matter of tuition and room and board. True, I had scraped through the first year, but year two stared me in the face – provided they let me back in.

So when my 19 year old ears heard Ken Pearsall tell me the Elijah and the widow woman and her son's story, and God's promise that he would provide, I believed it – a little bit, anyway – and determined to live my life on the basis of that promise. And I have, in varying degrees, ever since.

The second chapter in the spiritual memoir I wrote a few years back is titled, "The Promised Land" and is introduced with a phrase from the hymn we sang to open this service: "All I have needed, thy hand has provided; great is thy faithfulness." And what follows in that chapter is telling about how God has come through, first for my family of origin and then for me. Has it all been smooth sailing? Heavens no. Have all my needs been met according to my time schedule? No, not that either. But has all that I have really needed, been provided? Yes, it has been.

And that has been true in the lives of those that I have been privileged to preach to down through the years. A child dies at 7, a father at 42; two sons, one 19 the other 22, die a month apart – one murdered and the other in an auto accident – a divorce splits a family, a job is lost, a business fails, a favored child's train of life jumps the tracks – my goodness, how many there have been. And in all of these God came through, with just enough grace and strength for the living of those particular days; their jars of meal were never emptied and their jugs of oil never failed – just like Elijah promised.

So, if there is a central plank to my faith platform it is Elijah's promise – God would always be there for us – no matter.

It's the central message of the scriptures, isn't it? Even in the troubling times, when it looked as if all was lost, all wasn't lost. God was there – sometimes off in the shadows – but there, nonetheless.

> At the heart of the cyclone tearing the sky
> And flinging the cloud and the towers by,
> Is a place of central calm.
> So here in the roar of mortal things,
> I have a place where my spirit sings,
> In the hollow of God's palm.

Now this does not mean that you won't be anxious – afraid, even. I love the Sermon on the Mount, but I get my back up a bit when Jesus made it sound so easy – "take no thought for the morrow." Really," I want to say to Jesus, "on another day you told us that we better take some thought about the future, especially if we're planning on building something: we better sit down and count the cost before we start building – make sure we have enough set aside to finish the job." No, there will be anxious days, and times of doubt and wondering if we really have what it takes.

> It's not exactly courage
>   If you're not a bit afraid

> To climb the towering mountain
>   Or descend into the glade.
> But this is really courage,
>   At least I call it so,
> To say, "I fear that mountain.
>   But just the same, I'll go."

This may be why so many of us love the 23rd Psalm. Oh, I know it's probably the first bit of scripture we ever memorized. But we take hope in what it assures. Say it with me:

> The Lord is my shepherd, I shall not want.
> He maketh me to lie down in green pastures:
> He leadeth me beside the still waters,
> He restoreth my soul.
> He leadeth me in the paths of righteousness
> For his name's sake.
> Yea, though I walk through the valley of the shadow of death
> I will fear no evil:
> For thou art with me;
> Thy rod and thy staff they comfort me.
> Thou preparest a table before me
> In the presence of my enemies:
> Thou anointest my head with oil; my cup runneth over.
> Surely goodness and mercy shall follow me
> All the days of my life;
> And I will dwell in the house of the Lord forever.

A longtime friend of mine died this past week. He and I met in 1967 when he and his wife, newly-weds, showed up at St. Matthew's Church in Bowie, signed one of our "friendship pads" and I went to call on them. David and Jane joined and we became lifelong friends.

The two couples were senior high youth counselors for a while, our families had Christmas dinner together, I helped in his political campaign for the Maryland State Legislature, I baptized their children, we had season tickets for University of Maryland football games, and

Jane and Wave went to Folger's Theater to take in some Shakespeare plays.

Our families were close. Then David and Jane split up. No more Christmas dinners together but we stayed close. David became a judge. Then President Clinton appointed him to direct a federal office and when I retired I went to work for him as a speech writer.

David had battled diabetes all his life, so there were a series of heart attacks and by-pass surgery. Three years ago, David got an infection, then he had a stroke; the kids brought him back to Maryland from Florida and these last years have not been easy.

But through it all – and there has been a lot of "all" for the Ross family – David, Jane, Abbey and Justin have held on. Their faith has sustained them. And yesterday we were back in the church where we had met, the church David had helped me build. We were all there – Wave, Vicky, Tommy, Floyd, Jane, Abbey, Justin and David – in spirit – just like it had been for so many Christmases past; still there, singing the praises of our faith, and holding on, simply because we believe that our jars of meal will never be empty and our jugs of oil will never fail.

Faith Alters Appearances

Committing myself to being a lectionary preacher has forced me to deal with some scripture passages that normally I would not come anywhere near.

Like today's lessons: two out of the three fit that category. I could ignore those two except for the fact that the epistle lesson, which you did not hear, has Paul alluding to one of them in his letter to the church at Corinth.

The Gospel lesson is Luke's version of an incident in the life of Jesus that both Matthew and Mark also tell. It is an incident referred to as the Transfiguration, and since three of the Gospels tell about it, as does Peter in one of his letters, the early church decided to set aside a Sunday to commemorate it. And that Sunday is today.

The way Luke tells it – as do Matthew and Mark – Jesus took Peter, James and John with him to the top of a mountain to pray. And while he was praying his appearance changed: both his face and his clothes became dazzlingly white. His appearance changed. He was transfigured.

The writer of Exodus has a transfiguration story. But his main character is Moses. Like Jesus, Moses goes up on a mountain to talk with God and when he comes down his appearance has changed, too. "The skin of his face shown" is the way the scriptures describe it.

I would just as soon not have to deal with these stories, and you can probably guess why. Call me a liberal, a modernist, a progressive – call me what you will – I have trouble with out-of-the-ordinary occurrences.

I have no trouble letting you believe that every word in the Bible is true: that one day, back when, Joshua ordered the sun to stand still so that the Israelites could lay one on the Amorites, or, even, that God created the world in six calendar days. If you want to believe that, be my guest. I rather enjoy hearing some Iowa farmer rattle on about the UFO that landed in his corn field. With me, in most cases, it's believe and let believe. When it comes to the out-of-the ordinary occurrences in the Bible, I do not feel compelled to argue with anyone about whether or not they did happen. I just don't want to have to preach about them.

But when I read this part of Paul's second letter to the Church at Corinth, I thought I heard a word – even in these strange stories – that it wouldn't hurt us to hear. Listen to these words from today's epistle lesson:

> And all of us, with unveiled faces, seeing the glory of the Lord, as though reflected in a mirror, are being transformed into the same image from one degree of glory to another;

Faith alters appearances; contact with God – close contact – changes us; even our appearances.

Do you believe that? Do you suppose this is what we have been trying to say when we have quoted George Orwell's saying "at the age of 50 everyone gets the face they deserve;" that somehow who we are, how we live, the strength of our faith, gets reflected in our faces. Can people really tell, just by looking at us, that we have been in – spent a fair amount of time in – the presence of God? Does faith in God really change the way we look, or as Paul said in his letter, we "are being transformed from one degree of glory to another," or, as we sing ever and again,

> Filled with thy Spirit, 'til all shall see,
> Christ only always living in me.

The strong suggestion, it seems to me, is that faith does show; it can't be kept under wraps. Somewhere in the scriptures – I think it's in the book of Acts – there's this line: "they took knowledge of them that they had been with Jesus." You hang around Jesus – spend time in God's presence – and it's going to show.

But, in our appearances?

As I have told you, on occasion, I may not be the kind of journal keeper that Sue Collins has in mind for me to be, but I do jot things down – have been doing it for years – quotes, stories, articles, ideas. And in my sermon preparation I scan these notebooks. Here are some scribbles I found this week.

I had gone to one of our seminaries in California when I was on the General Board of Higher Education and Ministry. One day I was engaged in conversation with a minister from the East Ohio Conference. According to my notes she and I got into a conversation about our spiritual roots, and she began to talk about her grandmother – what a marvelous person she was – and she commented that her grand mom, though 81 (which, at that time seemed a ripe old age) didn't have a wrinkle in her face. When I asked if her grand mom was a person of faith, my friend said: "Is she a person of faith? She just glows with it."

I've known people like that. They wore their faith not so much on their sleeves but on their faces. Here's something that was written in a commentary about today's epistle lesson from Corinthians:

> It is a well-known principle that we become like what we look at. Our qualities of spirit are an unconscious reflection of those we admire in others. The inward change may even be revealed in our outward appearance.

What is being suggested is that our faith will be reflected in our appearances.

Could I make another suggestion – our faith will also show itself in our actions? We sing about this, too.

> They will know we are Christians by our love.

Our actions do speak louder than our words, and they ought to.

Mark Twain is quoted so often, I wonder if he really said all the things folks say he said. Anyway, the story is told that a Boston business tycoon told him one day that before he died he fully intended to travel to the Holy Land, climb to the top of Mt. Sinai, and read the Ten Commandments out loud. Twain is reported to have said: "I have a better idea. Why don't you stay home in Boston and live them?"

Two men were travelling on a train in England and one of them noticed a man sitting down the aisle a bit that he thought bore a striking resemblance to the Archbishop of Canterbury. He then said to his partner, "I bet you half a crown that that bloke over there is the Archbishop of Canterbury." His friend said, "I'll take your bet; I don't believe he is the archbishop."

So the man who made the wager got up, moved down the aisle and said to the passenger, "Pardon me, sir, but aren't you the Archbishop of Canterbury?" The man put down his paper, glared at this man he had never seen before, and said, "You get the blazes out of here and mind your own bloody business."

The man then went back to his friend and said, "The bet's off. We still don't know if he's the archbishop or not."

The low expectations for the behavior of archbishops held by the men in this story, notwithstanding, people ought to be able to get a read on our faith by the way we live our lives. Others should be able to know we are Christians, not just by our love, but how we behave.

It's not that I think every sermon should have three points but I would like to suggest another way our faith will show. Close contact with God – practicing the Presence – will affect the faith by which we live our lives.

Most of us Methodists have grown up knowing about John Wesley's Aldersgate experience. That was the night he went quite unwillingly to a Bible Study at a meeting house on Aldersgate Street in London. It was a boring study and Wesley, by his own admission, would much rather have stayed home. Someone was droning on, reading from Martin Luther's Preface to the Epistle to the Romans, and it was while that man was rattling on that Wesley felt his heart strangely warmed and he received his assurance that his sins were forgiven.

What we need to remember is that this assurance did not come at the beginning of Wesley's ministry. He had been preaching for some time, all the while not sure that he himself had faith. He made a trip to America to save the Indians, and, hopefully, in the process, save himself.

The assurance of his salvation didn't come while he was in America and on the voyage home a storm came up – a real typhoon type. The ship began to bob and weave and Wesley was petrified. Then he heard some singing. There were a bunch of Moravians on board singing hymns as they rode out the storm, resting in what Wesley perceived as assurance of God's presence, an assurance that eluded him.

Their faith shown – glowed, even, and Wesley saw it and shortly after he set foot on dry land he ended up at a boring Bible study on Aldersgate Street, and here we are today worshipping in a church that is part of a denomination that owes its existence to him, and who knows, to the faith of those Moravians that glowed in the dark of that stormed tossed sea.

Nathaniel Hawthorne wrote a short story that I was forced to read in a course I took in college on American Literature. The story is titled "The Great Stone Face."

It's about a little village in New England nestled between some gorgeous mountains. Etched in the side of one of the mountains is the figure of a man – a great stone face.

Growing up in that village is a boy named Ernest. He sits on his porch as his mother tells him the legend of the Great Stone Face. The legend goes back generations, and it says that one day a man will come to the village – a man of wisdom and honor – and he will bear the image of the Great Stone Face. So, Ernest grows up in the shadow of the Great Stone Face, waiting for the one who is to come.

A rich man comes and the village hopes he is the one. He isn't. A soldier comes but he isn't the one either, and neither is the next man who comes.

Ernest grows old, and, over the years, he has come to be known for his wisdom and honor – so much so that in the evenings people gather around him on the village common just to hear him share his wisdom.

A poet comes to the village and Ernest so wants him to be the one. As they gather on the common one evening for Ernest's sharing, suddenly the poet interrupts Ernest and shouts, "Look, Ernest himself bears the image of the Great Stone Face." Years of thinking on – gazing at – the image of the old man in the side of the mountain had caused Ernest to be like what he had looked at for so long.

How did Paul put it?

> Whatever is true, whatever is honorable, whatever is just, whatever is pure, whatever is lovely, whatever is gracious, think about these things.

And all three lessons for today make the same point: contact with God, being in God's presence, will change us – could even alter our appearances.

God's Neighborliness

I guess the best way to get me away from the Old Testament stories I love is to present me with a gospel story that I love a bit more.

The one for today is a rather well known one, at least for those of us who have been hanging around in places like this for a good bit of the time. It is usually one of the ones that we learned about early on in our Sunday school days. It is so well known that its title – the Good Samaritan – has established itself as a figure of speech and is probably used by a fair number of people who have no idea of its origins. It shows up in everyday conversations like "turn the other cheek" or "go the second mile."

The way Luke tells the story, a lawyer wanted to test Jesus. Notice how often it was a lawyer who wanted to "test" Jesus. What that really means is that he wanted to try and trip Jesus up – getting him to say something that might contradict religious tradition – casting doubt on his claim to be a valid spokesperson for God.

The lawyer asked a legitimate question: "What must I do to inherit eternal life?" So Jesus decided to test him – see if he knew what the law said. He did, and he quoted the ancient Shema: "You shall love the Lord your God with all your heart, and with all your soul, and with all your strength, and with all your mind, and your neighbor as yourself." Jesus gave him an A and an assignment: "Do this and you will live."

But this test wasn't going the way the lawyer wanted it to go. Luke says he "wanted to justify himself." I am not sure what Luke had in mind by using the phrase "justify himself." It seems to mean that he wasn't ready to give up on his attempt to trip Jesus up. So he asks: "And just who is my neighbor?"

That may not seem a loaded question to you but it was back in that day. This was a heavily segregated society. Boundaries were drawn. Each person had a place. Jews, Gentiles, Men, Women, and the lowest of the low were the Samaritans. Samaritans were the scum of the earth – mixed breeds who were considered unclean – not fit for human society. So the lawyer wanted to know just who from this separated bunch was he supposed to be neighborly to.

What a masterful story teller Jesus was. "A man was going down from Jerusalem to Jericho and fell into the hands of robbers." Doesn't give the man a label – he could have been a Jew or a gentile – Jesus doesn't say. Whoever he was he got waylaid on this treacherous strip of road, known for its ambushes.

Now Jesus begins to tack on some labels. A priest was heading down that road – maybe he wore the clerical garb of that day and felt safe – and when he saw this bloodied and beaten man by the side of the road he didn't just walk by him – ignoring his wounded condition – he crossed over to the other side of the road.

Then, Jesus went on, a Levite came along. Levites were sort of lesser priests – maybe something like our deacons. But he, like the priest who had come along ahead of him, passed by the beat up guy, and also, like the priest, crossed over to the other side of the road.

And then – I hope Jesus paused, just for effect – along came a Samaritan, one of the despised ones. He didn't cross over to the other side of the road like the two Holy Joes before him had done. No siree. "He went to him," is the way Luke says Jesus characterized the Samaritan's response, bandaged the man's wounds, poured oil and wine on them; put him on his own animal and walked along beside until they got to an inn. There he took care of the beaten man, and gave the innkeeper an amount of money equal to two days wages to be used for any further care that might be necessary, and, would you believe it, said to the innkeeper, when I stop back by in a few days, if his care has cost you anymore, I'll square that up with you.

One of you sent me one of these internet pieces that make the rounds. This one was a listing of incidents that ended with, "and you could have heard a pin drop." I bet you that when Jesus finished that story, you could have heard a pin drop.

Then Jesus fixed his stare on the lawyer and asked him which of these three do you think was a neighbor to the man who fell into the hands of the robbers? And when the lawyer said "the one who showed him mercy" – maybe he just couldn't bring himself to say "the Samaritan" – Jesus didn't make a fuss over that; he just said, "Go and do likewise."

Hearing this story read to you today probably doesn't fit the "you could have heard a pin drop category." But doesn't it still have a word for us?

Take the central point Jesus was trying to make by choosing a social outcast as the hero of the story. Isn't that the way God operates? He turns things around. "The last shall be first, and the first last." "Not everyone who says 'Lord, Lord' will enter the kingdom; but he who does the will of the father." We think we can know who the holy ones are. But we can't, really. By putting a Samaritan in the starring role of this story, Jesus shatters social boundaries and class divisions. No one, no group, is to be despised or cast aside. "He hath made of one blood all nations."

And shouldn't we church people pause a bit to give some attention to the villains in this story: the church people – the members of the religious establishment. They didn't just pass by the beaten up guy, they crossed over to the other side of the road. Maybe they had bigger fish to fry. Who knows?

But we present day followers of Jesus better sit up and take notice. Reading our Bibles and worshipping together is important; more important than some of us seem to think. But there are folks out there lying beside some road somewhere who need some ministering to.

Some of us old Methodist preacher warhorses grouse a bit from time to time; talk about the old days – how we did it. And one of our concerns is the lessening emphasis that we see being given to what we used to call "social concerns." At sessions of annual conference there would be lots of talk about poverty, unemployment and racial injustice. We seemed to think that Jesus wanted us to pay some attention to the least and the lost. And not just our conference, but the denomination itself, quite often led by our bishops, kept social justice concerns on the front burner.

It just doesn't seem the same to some of us well-worn preacher types. We go to conference and all the talk seems to be about church growth – concern about our dwindling numbers – and personal spiritual development. And, oh yes, much concern about forms of worship that might attract the younger crowd. Not many discussions about how best to be a neighbor to the bruised and bleeding lying beside our present day roads.

I know this is going to sound political but when you get to be eighty you ought to be cut a little slack. I get more than just perturbed, I get angry, when some of the Tea Party types – many of whom seem to be the guardians of the morals of this country and claim, a lot of them, to be born again Christians – march against our country's attempt to try and see to it that those among us, who are broken and lying beside life's highways, have access to health insurance. They stick the president's name on the Affordable Care Act – tapping into the personal resentment toward our duly elected president – and seem quite content to do as the priest and the Levite in Jesus' story did, walk right on by.

I don't know the answer – maybe the Affordable Care Act Law that was passed isn't the answer. But we who claim Christ's name have to be on the side of those who want to try and find ways to be the Good Samaritan, and go to the ones lying by the side of life's road and not cross over to the other side of the road.

Remember the lawyer's initial question, asking what he had to do to inherit eternal life; remember Jesus' answer: "Do this and you will live." Then there was the second question about who the neighbor was, and Jesus told him to "go and do likewise."

Notice that there was no promise of any reward to the lawyer for being a good neighbor. Here's a comment I read on this passage:

"The duty of neighborliness transcends any calculation of reward. The Samaritan could not have expected any reward or payment for what he did for the beaten man. Mercy sees only need and responds with compassion."

I think most of us here accept Jesus' great summation of the law: we are to love God with our heart and soul and mind and strength, and our neighbor as ourselves. And who is our neighbor – they all are. But more importantly, the takeaway from today's story is not so much determining who my neighbor is, but rather, to whom am I being a neighbor. In God's sight, at least according to the Good Samaritan story, a neighbor is one who, like the lawyer said, the one who shows mercy.

There's an Arab proverb that says, "To have a good neighbor you must be one."

Is the Lord Among Us

In the Exodus lesson for today the children of Israel are complaining again. Last week – the lesson you didn't hear – it was nothing to eat. This week it's nothing to drink.

So they put it to Moses, their tour guide, whom, they think, leaves a good deal to be desired. "What say, O fearless leader? Why did you bring us out of Egypt, to kill us and our children and our livestock with thirst? Yeah, the manna is all right, but what happens if we all just dry up and blow away?"

Well, Moses got them some water – change that. The story says God did. God had to remind Moses of the power of his staff – the one that had stood him in good stead in previous days. So, Moses struck a rock with that staff and they had plenty of water to drink.

Moses named the spot where all this happened Massah and Meribah – which means test and quarrel. It was his opinion that the children of Israel had been testing God and just throwing a hissy fit.

Well, I want to give these wandering Jews a bit of slack. You see, I've been there and done that. And I think you have as well. So I want to take seriously their plaintive lament – "Is the Lord among us or not?"

Am I right in assuming that you have been there? No, I'm not talking about being without water. I'm talking about being in some strange place – a place where you have never been before – a situation that is different t from anything you have ever known. All the old familiar landmarks are gone. The maps you have always used to check out directions – well, the road you are now on doesn't seem to be anywhere on that old well worn, dog-eared map. And it's scary. And if you are a person of faith, and have come to depend on God being somewhere around, perhaps the question does cross your mind, "Is the Lord among us or not?"

Years later some of these folks' descendants would be in some other strange place – wandering around – and so they hung their harps up on the trees and stopped singing, giving as their reason that the Lord's songs weren't that easy to sing in strange and distant lands.

So, I don't find these Hebrew children's question either quarrelsome or petulant. It seems rather human to me, since, as I said, I've been there and done that.

I am in one of those places now. I have lived believing that we – you and I – live in a blessed land: purple mountain majesties above the fruited plane and all that. I grew up being told that a family mired in poverty in Tennessee could, if they worked at it, find a way out and house, feed and clothe a family, and seeing my family do just that.

But also watching other families do the same thing. I lived during a time when we came together as a nation and, using grit and determination, fought and won over despotic powers in the world. I have lived through a missile crisis when we came, oh so close, to nuclear war. I have lived through a presidential assassination, race riots, economic recessions, savings and loan scandals, the list seems endless. And in all of these my basic faith that we, as a country, would make it through – so help us God.

But, now, that confidence is being sorely tested. We seem so divided as a country – so unwilling to give a little take a little – which is the essence of a democracy. We are in an unsettled place as a country – with tremendous challenges facing us – a lot at stake, and I don't see any willingness to come together as "one nation, under God" – a willingness that in days past seemed rather automatic. I have lived believing that "we shall overcome" but right now I am not all that sure.

So, I feel for those children of Israel when they asked, plaintively, I think, "is the Lord among us or not?"

And I know some of you have been there and done that; maybe not wandering in a strange land like I have just described – my strange land of worrying about my country – but in other strange lands. I know this because I have met people along the way for whom this has been true.

The scripts in these life stories vary, but the plots are the same: a companion of many years dies, or, sometimes, just walks out; a child is buried; a job is lost; a trust is betrayed; a business goes belly up; a reduction in force occurs and the old job just isn't there anymore. It happens, and the terrain shifts. Old landmarks are gone, and we do wonder – at least those of us who have come to depend on God wonder – "Is the Lord among us or not?"

You see what I am suggesting: there are times when, because of changed circumstances, shifting situations, that God seems absent. Bill Coffin when he was pastor at Riverside Church in New York City lost his 24 year old son when the car he was driving plunged into the Charles River in Boston. Ten days after that tragedy Dr. Coffin preached in his church and told his congregation that one of the realities of grief is the absence of God. And he cited Jesus as an example, who, you will remember, called to mind as he hung on the cross, that ancient psalm which reads, "My God, My God, why hast thou forsaken me?"

And what we really want, and need, in such times is to know that God hasn't forsaken us, or, as the Hebrew children put it, "Is the Lord among us or not?"

Henry Lyte wasn't doing too well in his pastorates. For some reason he never seemed to make it with his parishioners. He dabbled some in poetry and one day he sat down and wrote:

> Abide with me; fast falls the eventide;

> The darkness deepens, Lord with me abide.

> When other helpers fail and comforts flee,
>
> Help of the helpless, O, abide with me.

Woody Allen put it humorously when he said he wished God would give him some clear sign that He was around – like making a large deposit in his name in a Swiss bank.

But it isn't that simple. And a fair number of voices say God isn't anywhere around. Mark Twain said once that God doesn't even know we are here. And Lily Tomlin said on one occasion, "We are in this alone."

But most of us – even though we wonder – sometimes – like the little girl who prayed, "Our father who art in New Haven, how do you know my name?" – and ask the same question the children of Israel asked – "Is the Lord among us or not" – at least those of us who have come to depend on God's presence in our lives – keep hoping and trusting that God is with us and among us.

Which is what Bill Coffin goes on to say in that sermon he preached ten days after his son drowned in the Charles River. Listen to what he wrote:

> "My, My God, why hast thou forsaken me?" Yes, but at least, "My God, My God," and the Psalm doesn't end that way."

And now for the epistle lesson for today: it's in a letter Paul wrote to the church at Philippi. It's his promise to us for this day. Did you hear it?

> Work out your own salvation with fear and trembling;
> for it is God who is at work in you, enabling you both
> to will and to work for his good pleasure.

This is our hope, isn't it, that God is at work in us, even in those times; times when we are traveling in some uncharted territory; times when we wonder if God is still around. Paul says he is still around, even in this strange place; so we make this truth our own.

Thomas Starnes

One of my favorite writers is Frederich Buechner. You will get tired of me quoting him, but that won't stop me from doing it. Listen to what he wrote once about faith:

> In my own experience, the ways God appears in our lives are elusive and ambiguous always. There is always room for doubt in order, perhaps, that there will always be room to breathe. There is so much in life that hides God and denies the very possibility of God that there are times when it is hard not to deny God altogether. Yet it is possible to have faith, nonetheless. Faith is that nonetheless."

He also wrote, on another occasion, "Faith is a way of seeing in the dark."

And this is the hope we live by – you and I: that even when we are called to travel in some strange and distant land, and it occurs to us to wonder if God is still with us, we remember Paul's words of assurance that God is still at work in us, and we remember to tack on Buechner's word, nonetheless.

The Hound of Heaven

I sort of apologized last week for constantly turning to these ancient Hebrew stories for sermon material, and so wanted not to do that today.

And I thought I might be able to bring that off since the Jonah story has never been a favorite of mine. Oh, it's a good story. A bit of a stretch, what with the whole whale bit:. how could Jonah have possibly escaped the ravages of whale gastric juices – but a pretty good story nonetheless.

But what really is the point of the story, and why was it selected to be a part of the canon of Holy Scripture? Not all of the stories submitted for publication got past the editors' desk. How did this one make the cut?

But the epistle lesson left me cold – Paul going on about a subject he knew absolutely nothing about – marriage; he even said he didn't. And the gospel lesson is a very brief mention of Jesus beginning to select his disciples. Mark doesn't waste words, so I will wait for one of the other gospel writers' version of this critical part of the Jesus story.

So I put the lessons aside and went on about my business, practicing some of the "pre-paper thought" that I learned about in a college course on creative writing.

And I remembered something: an old sermon that I had preached on Jonah. I really thought that I had never preached a Jonah sermon. And as far as dishing one up on a Sunday morning that is true. But this was a sermon that I preached to a class I was taking in seminary on literature and the Bible.

I have no idea where that sermon is – or even if it is stored away in any box somewhere. And what I remember about what I said is precious little. But what is filed away, wherever things like that get filed is the notion that I talked a lot about God in it.

For instance, I must have talked about God's pursuit of us. The reason I know this is that I quoted for the first time Francis Thompson's classic poem, *The Hound of Heaven*. Francis Thompson died in 1907. He had been an opium addict, and God just wouldn't leave him alone. So he wrote about it.

> I fled Him, down the nights and down the days;
>   I fled Him, down the arches of the years;
>   I fled Him, down the labyrinthine ways
>   Of my own mind; and in the midst of tears
>   I hid from Him, and under running laughter.
>   Up vistaed hopes I sped;
>   And shot, precipitated,
>   Adown Titanic glooms of chasmed fears,
>   From those strong feet that followed after.

The Hound of Heaven caught up with Francis Thompson just as He did with Jonah. According to the story, it took some temporary confinement in the belly of a whale to get Jonah to do God's bidding – go to Ninevah, that wicked city, and preach the word – but, in the end, the Hound of Heaven got his man.

This is the first thing about Jonah's God. He just won't let us go. We sing about this "love that will not let us go," and some of us have experienced it. The stories differ. Sometimes we betray our better selves, and we head down a path that we know will lead to no good end, and yet we keep on going. And so does God keep on going, right after us, trying to get us to return to those better selves that we know, deep down, are our true selves. How did the Psalmist put it: "If I make my bed in hell, thou art there."

So the first word about Jonah's God is that he will not let us go. We may try to flee his presence, like Jonah, but in the stillness of some night,

No One Knows When It's a Good Day

or, perhaps, when we hear the strains of an old hymn, we might also hear the steady beat of those strong feet that Francis Thompson wrote about, following after us.

The other thing I remember from this old sermon is that I made a big deal about Jonah getting all bent out of shape when God destroyed the bush that he had been sulking beneath.

Jonah was sulking because God had spared Ninevah from destruction. Now, mind you, God spared Ninevah because they had turned from their wicked ways, as Jonah had preached to them to do. Then why on earth was Jonah angry?

Well, he answers that question in the beginning verses of chapter 4. Jonah tells God that the reason he didn't want to go to Ninevah in the first place was because he knew that God "was gracious and merciful, slow to anger, and abounding in steadfast love, and ready to relent from punishing."

So, the story is that Jonah took God's message to Ninevah, but he really, really, hoped that the Ninevites would pay no attention to him – continue in their wickedness – and God would zap them. But Jonah was a better communicator than he thought; the people listened, obeyed and God spared the city. And Jonah got mad, pouted, and even asked God to put him out of his misery.

The only insight I have in Jonah's behavior, and it is minimal, is that he reminds me of some of the hell fire evangelists I heard as a kid. It seems that they loved the whole doom and gloom, eternal punishment part of the old, old, story, more than they loved the God is merciful, slow to anger part of the story.

But I am not here to analyze Jonah. My focus is Jonah's God, and that picture is clearer.

"Jonah," God says, "Is it right for you to be angry about the bush?" God can't believe his ears when Jonah responds, "you better believe I'm angry – angry enough to die."

Then God unloads: "You are concerned about the bush, for which you did not labor and which you did not grow; it came into being in a night and perished in a night. And should I not be concerned about Ninevah, that great city, in which there are more than a hundred and twenty thousand persons who do not know their right hand from their left, and also many animals."

This is the book of Jonah's God: a God who, as we also sing on occasion, has the whole world in His hands. The tiny little baby, the wind and the rain, everybody, and even, according to the book of Jonah, the animals. And did you catch that strange line – a city of a hundred and twenty thousand persons who do not know their right hand from their left hand. Supposedly that's an idiomatic saying of that time for people who are morally and spiritually unaware.

So Jonah's God says that he cares for everybody. Just like we sing each Sunday,

> Jesus loves the little children,
>   All the children of the world.
>   Red and yellow, black and white,
>   They are precious in his sight.

Jonah's God says that all are precious: those we call "illegals", or those who bow at a different altar, and yes, it still needs to be said, those whose skin doesn't match ours.

Jonah's God takes us all in. And truth is – we can't get away – the hound of heaven won't let us.

Life's Ups and Downs

The last time we heard anything from Elijah was a couple Sundays ago when he was basking in the glory of his triumph over the prophets of Baal. I guess he showed them whose God was the stronger: it was God, Jehovah, who sent down fire from heaven and consumed the sacrifice – the water-soaked sacrifice – on the altar. So there, take that, you followers of this pagan god.

The Elijah we meet today is not that same heroic figure of a couple weeks ago. Jezebel, the tyrant queen, has put the fear of God into him. When Ahab, her husband, tells her that Elijah has slain all the prophets of Baal, even though she isn't the king, she sends word to Elijah that she is going to do to him what he has done to her prophets. And what does Elijah the fearless prophet of the most-high God do – he turns tail and runs.

You know one of the reasons why I take the scriptures seriously? They let it all hang out – even with their heroic figures. Elijah is one of the Biblical heroes. He has a place in Israel's history. To this day a seat for him is reserved at the Seder meal table. They could have left this part of the story out, and left in our minds the picture of Elijah standing on Mt. Carmel, sword held high, victor over the prophets of Baal.

The tellers of God's story didn't need to tell us about David's lust for Bathsheba and his arranging to have her husband killed so that she might become his queen. Did we really need to know that Peter, on that night to end all nights, lied, not once but three times, telling that young girl that he had no idea who Jesus was.

Maybe we didn't really need to know that Elijah's knees buckled when a queen with fire in her eyes sent a few of her hit men to take him down. But we do know it; so what are we going to make of this part of God's story.

Well, let's see if it's just a dusty old story from a long ago time, or if, just maybe, it has a word or two for us.

I couldn't come up with anything better as a title for this sermon than life's ups and downs. The story today is about a down time for Elijah. He had been riding high and now he was cowering in some corner fearing for his life. What happened?

Who knows really? But we can make an educated guess – based on what we have come to know about human nature. Down times seem to come to us all at one time or another and they sometimes follow on the heels of our up times. Maybe our up times have involved hard work or stress – up times, it has been proved, are stressful in and of themselves – but we are down. Of course Elijah had Jezebel after him, but it had to be more than that. Was she really more of a threat than the 850 prophets of Baal that he had squared off against? Whatever the reason, Elijah this mighty man of God was down, and if the story were being written today the word used to describe Elijah's condition would be depressed.

And God comes after him. Elijah has camped out in a wilderness and is sitting under a broom tree contemplating ending it all except he wants God to do the deed for him. He deserves to die, he tells God, because he is no better than his ancestors. God doesn't assist his suicide – he lets him sleep it off – then God sends an angel to wake him up and tell him to eat something.

Let's pause here for a moment. Elijah's scared – has an angry queen after him – suffering from an anxiety induced depressive state – and the best advice God has for him is to eat something.

I was the recipient of such advice back some years ago. It was a time of psychic struggle for me. Bouts of anxiety had dogged my tracks for years. Objects of that anxiety had floated about, fixing its self on various things that I could obsess about. Most of this didn't really interfere with my life, but now it was getting in the way of what I was doing as a living: my anxieties centered on my standing up in the pulpit and preaching. Those twenty or so minutes that I spent sermonizing had become white-knuckle times for me.

I was in therapy at the time with a God-sent therapist, Bob Kirsch. I was convinced that this pulpit anxiety of mine was proof positive that I was not really called to preach but was merely doing what I thought my daddy wanted me to do. One day, Dr. Kirsch said, "Tom, what do you eat for breakfast on Sunday?" Not seeing any reason for the question, I answered it, nonetheless. "Well, I eat a sweet roll or a doughnut and have two or three cups of coffee." "Next Sunday morning," Dr. Kirsch suggested, "Eat an egg and a piece of toast and drink a glass of milk." I didn't preach any better after that, but my knees stopped buckling and before long – especially after an organist of mine told me after the service that I was doing what God had in mind for me to do – I accepted the fact that preaching was my calling and kept right on, including this very morning, eating an egg and toast for my Sunday morning breakfast.

I am not trying to play Dr. Oz. I'm only suggesting that this old story about Elijah's down time, and God's first word to him is to eat something, can be instructive for us. Our bodies affect our minds and our moods. So when your down time comes, make sure you eat right. Not too much, mind you; down times can cause us to eat more than we should. It's just that the word in this story about Elijah needing to eat when life was closing in on him is a word we need to hear.

And it worked. Not right off, because he lay back down and took a nap so the angel had to revisit him, wake him up and tell him to eat some more. He did and on the strength of that he set out on a forty day and forty night hike to Horeb, the mount of God, where he crawled into his shell again. This time he didn't cower under a tree; he held up in a cave.

The next morning God was his wake-up call. It isn't clear whether God came or whether it was an angel; all the scriptures say is that it was the word of the Lord that came to him. And the word from God was a question. A simple one: "What are you doing here?" Elijah blabbers out some self-pitying excuses: "I have been very zealous for the Lord, unlike a lot of other Israelites who have forsaken your covenant, thrown down your altars and killed your prophets." And then he moaned, "I alone am left." Whine, whine, whine.

And God would have none of it. This time he didn't tell Elijah to grab a bite to eat. He told him to go out and stand on the mountain before the Lord because the Lord was about to pass by. Elijah went and stood on the mount and there was a great wind that split mountains and broke rocks, but Elijah saw no traces of the Lord. And after the wind there was an earthquake, but the Lord wasn't in that either. Then came a period of deathly silence and old spooked Elijah headed back to the cave. But God wouldn't let him in. He had another suggestion. This time it wasn't you need to eat something. This time God's word was: you need to get busy. Head down to Damascus; I have an assignment for you.

Elijah went and, as God had commanded, he anointed a couple kings and laid hands on his prophetic successor, Elisha.

One of my favorite preachers from my beginning days as a preacher was Harry Emerson Fosdick, the many years pastor of the famed Riverside Church in New York City. He had a line in one of his sermons that I have never forgotten. He said:

> It is easier to act our way into a new way of thinking,
> than to think ourselves into a new way of acting.

How tempting it is, when the down times come, to hold our own little pity party – sit under our broom tree equivalent or crawl into the closest thing we have to a cave – and wonder why life has dealt us this particular hand. What we need to hear on our down days are God's word to Elijah, "get busy, I have something for you to do," and Dr. Fosdick's words suggesting that it is easier to act ourselves into a new way of thinking than it is to think ourselves into a new way of acting.

When I got to this point in my writing, I felt a need to add a footnote: I hope none of you have heard me minimizing the fears and anxieties that are so much a part of the human condition and are part and parcel of so many of our "down days," and heard me suggesting that eating right and scurrying around keeping busy is all that is needed to quieten the deepest fears in our souls. I have not meant to suggest that.

So let me end with something I heard this week. My favorite living preacher – Fosdick has been dead for a number of years – is Frederick Buechner, who will be 87 in July. Buechner writes, and speaks, so movingly about suffering and fear and faith – all written out of his own struggles with anxiety. When he was nine years old, he was awakened one Saturday morning by a commotion downstairs in the driveway, and he, and his younger brother Jamie, went over to the window and saw their father's feet sticking out of the garage. Life was too tough for his Dad to try and make sense of anymore. I discovered a web site of Buechner's this this week and heard a bit of a lecture. He was lecturing on the fear of death and he told this story.

He was on a plane and, being, as he said, a not completely relaxed flyer, the rather serious bit of turbulence they encountered unnerved him, to say the least. Trays of food and drink were flying every which way, and in the midst of his fear, came these old words from Deuteronomy: "Underneath are the everlasting arms." He sat back in his seat, assured by these old words that underneath him, those 30,000 or so feet up, were some everlasting arms that would not let him go.

This is where my faith rests. On my down days when eating right doesn't cut it and finding plenty to do doesn't either, I pray the serenity prayer and then turn it over to a loving heavenly father who has promised never to leave me nor forsake me.

Soul Struggles

The Biblical story of Jacob wrestling with some unknown figure in the dead of night is a familiar one to most church goers. Perhaps not as familiar as the other night time episode Jacob experienced when he dreamed of a ladder reaching from earth to heaven – an experience that we have – most of us church people anyway – sung about down through the years: "We are climbing Jacob's ladder."

Charles Wesley wrote a hymn about this wrestling match of Jacob's. It was never a congregational favorite – and certainly isn't now when the emphasis seems to be on using more contemporary music – because it's long and its tune is hardly singable.

> Come, O Thou Traveler unknown, whom still I hold, but cannot see.
> My Company before is gone, and I am left alone with thee.

Wesley's second verse is instructive. It tells the nature of this crisis event in Jacob's life.

> I need not tell thee who I am, my misery and sin declare;
> Thyself hast called me by my name, look on thy hands and read it there.

For Jacob this seems to have been the mother of all soul struggles. Was it his mid-life crisis or was it some full-blown battle to determine his identity? Will the real Jacob, son of Isaac and Rebekah, brother of Esau, please stand up?

It could have been an identity crisis. Jacob must have wondered who he was. Was he, at heart, a cheat – to his own brother, even? And in his day – doing what he had done – had put his mother at risk of being cursed. Or was he one of God's own, as the Lord in the ladder dream seemed to indicate. It was a soul struggle of some sort, a passage to end all passages, what some came to call a dark night of the soul. Jacob wrestled and won. In the ladder story the place where Jacob slept got a new name – Bethel. In this story of the wrestling match it was Jacob who got a new name – Israel. He had struggled and won; he was a new person.

There are differing opinions as to the identity of Jacob's wrestling partner. Some interpreters of this legend see Jacob's opponent as the River God who stood between Jacob and the land of Israel. Some wonder if it weren't his brother, Esau. Various psychologists want to write it down as Jacob having a go of it with himself – doing battle with his own inner demons. Jacob felt, at least as I read the story, that he had taken on none other than Yahweh himself. As the story tells it:

> "So Jacob called the place Peniel, saying, 'For I have seen God face to face.'"

In order to try and make it easy on myself, I want to combine two of the above options. I think it was a struggle with himself – a coming to terms with who he really was – but also a struggle with God, simply because I happen to believe that in our coming to terms with who we are – in our soul struggles – God is right there in the mix with us. Further, I want to suggest that when we find ourselves, or come closer to finding ourselves, we increase the chances of our ever discovering the God of our understanding.

So let me take this old story and make a couple points about our own soul struggles.

And the first is that they usually occur at dark; not necessarily in the evening hours, but in those times that St. John of the Cross labelled dark nights of the soul.

They are that – these times of struggle; not a lot of light present. What I want to suggest, though, is that if we care at all about soul-growth, or coming to terms with who we are, we better learn "to bless darkness."

That's a phrase out of Kahlil Gibran's <u>Prophet</u>. The Prophet is giving his farewell before he sails from Orphalese back to the isle of his birth, and he says:

> But you do not see, nor do you hear, and it is well,
> The veil that clouds your eyes shall be lifted by the hands that wove it,
> Yet you shall not deplore having known blindness, nor regret having been deaf.
> And you shall bless darkness as you would bless light.

"No pain, no gain," is the way we sloganize it. Frederich Buechner says it much better: "We are never more in touch with life than when life is painful." F. W. Robertson, the Buechner of the 19th century, who struggled with his own demons of depression, and preached such marvelous sermons, said: "There is a sense in which darkness has more of God than light has."

There is a wealth of quotes like this. Joseph Campbell, the mythologist, expressed it this way:

> One thing that comes out in myths is that at the bottom of the abyss comes the voice of salvation. The black moment is the moment when the real message of transformation is going to come. At the darkest moment comes the light.

Meister Eckhart said: "Truly, it is in the darkness that one finds the light, so when we are in sorrow, then this light is nearest of all to us."

This old story out of Jacob's life has the Spirit out at night because that's what they believed: spirits only roamed the earth at night. That may or not be so; what I do believe is so – as do the people I have been quoting – is that quite often it takes a dark night experience to put us in touch with who we really are, and give us at least a fighting chance to come face to face with the eternal One.

Darkness is my first point; determination is the second. Here's some more of that Wesley hymn I began with on Jacob wrestling.

> With thee all night I mean to stay,
> And wrestle till the break of day.

Jacob held on. He told, whoever it was, "I will not let you go.

Dark nights – soul struggle times – do some folks in. Drinking gets a bit heavy for a few – quieten those demons down; a lot easier than wrestling – at least at the outset. Some choose other destructive ways to act out; anything to avoid a real life and death soul struggle. Some decide to cash it all in, feeling that the struggles of the soul are just too much to bear. God is there, in the darkness, as is our only chance for a new life; but it takes two to wrestle and that requires determination.

There is a word of hope in this story – an obvious word: Jacob made it through. It was hard work, to be sure, but he made it. The wrestling scarred him for life – never walked the same afterwards. And we won't walk the same, either, if we hold on – fight it out.

One other thing and I'm back to Buechner. He said in one of his books, "Faith is a way of seeing in the dark," and in another, "Anyone who has ever known him has known him perhaps better in the dark than anywhere else, because it is in the dark where he seems to visit us most often."

This is our hope: God is there, in those dark nights of ours, hanging on with us, holding us up, even; while at the same time wrestling with us – not wanting us to give in too easily – until we come through the struggle; a changed person, who will, from here on out, walk in a decidedly different manner.

What a Heaven's For

Heaven is a word I do not often use. Even at memorial services I do not use it a lot. I will say it when it turns up in scriptures that I am reading. But when I am using my own words, I don't often use it.

More often than not I find myself affirming a belief in everlasting life. I love to quote from the 8th chapter of Romans that nothing – in life or in death – can ever separate us from God's love. I have been known to mention more than just a few times that life is the lord of death. But, on my own, I generally don't use the word heaven.

I'm not sure why. I love to scan for "family" radio stations in hopes of hearing one of my favorites, and not long ago I hit on Willie Nelson, of all people, singing,

> There's a land that is fairer than day,
> And by faith we can see it afar.
> For the father waits over the way,
> To prepare us a dwelling place there.
> In the sweet by and by . . . .

I grew up on songs like that – songs about heaven.

> When we all get to heaven –
> What a day of rejoicing that will be.

The church that nurtured me in the faith – the preachers I listened to – didn't seem to care all that much about this world. To hear them talk this world was a wicked and sinful place – heaven was the preferred location.

Well, I didn't feel all that unkindly toward this old world. It seemed like a pretty good place to me – even the little bit of it that I had seen from the rather limited vantage point of Sussex County, Delaware, in those pre-Bay bridge days. Heaven probably was an okay place, but if I had my druthers, I wasn't quite ready to go there.

Heaven was also part of a package deal in the church I grew up in. You couldn't talk about heaven without talking about hell. In that particular church world I hung around in, you couldn't have one without the other.

So, I could never get all that excited about streets of gold, walls of jasper or gates of pearl. For in the "sweet by and by" we sang about; when the roll would finally be called up yonder, some might walk on streets of gold, but the not so lucky ones (and I always saw myself in this not-so-select company) would have to head for those nether regions that lay somewhere east of Eden.

For whatever reason, I haven't talked all that much about heaven. Nor have many of my moderate to liberal preacher friends. Even those who didn't grow up on the "good news of hell," as I did, have studiously avoided talking about heaven. "None of this 'pie in the sky by and by' business for us; the kingdom is now, right here; so let's get busy."

But, there's the church year, and the scripture readings that roll around each Sunday, and certain days to commemorate articles of our faith, and one of those certain days happens to be today, All Saints, with a suggested lesson that uses the word I have so studiously avoided: Heaven.

I remind myself of the man who said that he spent twenty years trying to come to terms with his doubts. Then one day it dawned on him that he had better come to terms with his faith. It was then, as he put it, that he passed from the agony of questions that he couldn't answer into the agony of answers he couldn't escape.

I have my questions about heaven – still, after all these years – but it is a word – a metaphor, maybe – that suggests some answers I can no longer escape. So, on this All Saints Sunday let me suggest two or three.

The first is that there is more to life than this. I do believe this much. No, I am not prepared to go into great detail about what lies beyond. I share Reinhold Niebuhr's view that we must not claim too much when it comes to knowledge of the great beyond. He said one time in a lecture titled, "Mystery and Meaning" that those who claim to know too much can be divided into two groups: there are those who claim to know so much that they deny any existence beyond history. Then there are those – the religious ones – who "know the geography of heaven and of hell, and the furniture of the one and the temperature of the other." Niebuhr says that a genuine Christian faith moves between the two. Then he adds: but we can know enough to know that "all known existence points beyond itself."

This is where I am. I do not know whether the streets in heaven are paved with gold or even if there are streets. I have no idea whether hell has flames or even if there is such a place. What I do believe, deep in my soul, is that this world is not all there is.

And it's this notion – this article of faith – that we need to hold on to. Maslov said once that if the only tool you have is a hammer then you tend to treat everything as if it were a nail. If you think that this world is all that there is, and your three score and ten, more or less, is all that there is, then why not eat drink and be merry. And if the market collapses and you lose everything then why not grab a gun and shoot your broker, because in your mind you've lost everything.

If this is all that there is, that does do something to your hopes, your dreams, and your values. But those of us who gather in places like this each week, that all appearances in the world, notwithstanding, there is more to us than just a bunch of molecules or whatever it is that makes up our bodies. There is a deeper dimension to us, and, as Niebuhr put it, "all known existence points beyond itself."

This is the first thing I am clear about when it comes to the word heaven.

The second is something that Immanuel Kant said. He said that he believed in something beyond – a heaven, sort of – because God had to have a chance to balance the books.

Now, I have to be careful here. Final judgment scenarios don't do it for me: giant ledgers being opened and treasuries of merit being cashed in – all that turns me off. But, what about a need for a "wrap-up;" that hunger for a conclusion that matches – at least for the person of faith – the "in the beginning" part of the story? Isn't there a need to see how it all turns out? Is life a soap opera that never ends? Will the world turn forever?

Couldn't this be what is meant by all the Biblical talk about that Great Day of the Lord when "every knee shall bow and every tongue confess" and all hidden things shall be brought to light?

Isn't there something in us that cries out for some kind of ultimate justice? Not so that the rascals will finally get theirs – but, as Kant said – a kind of balancing of the books. Life isn't fair. Bad things happen to good people and vice versa. Rain falls on just and unjust alike. The good die young. Evil prospers. Nice guys finish last. That's life. Isn't there a need for some kind of cosmic wrap-up – some marvelously creative ending to match the marvelously creative beginning?

No, I don't know how it will be. I just feel it will be. And, for me, the word heaven keeps this hope alive.

The third answer that I can't escape has to do with the word home: Heaven as home.

I am forever trying to justify my moderate addiction to sports to my wife. She, the intellectual, can't understand how on earth anyone as intelligent, as she insists I am, could possibly read the sports pages first in the morning paper.

So, when the late Bart Giamatti's book came out a few years back, I got a copy and read parts of it to her. But you need a little background.

Bart Giamatti was an intellectual. A renaissance scholar elected president of Yale when he was 38. But his first love was baseball and he left Yale to become president of the National Baseball League and then elected Commissioner of baseball.

His book that I bought and read to Wave to upgrade her view of my smarts, or lack thereof, is a series of lectures he gave at the University of Michigan, titled <u>Take Time For Paradise.</u>

As I am reading along, in his final lecture, where he is talking about the layout of the baseball diamond, I come to the part where he is talking about home plate, and he is wondering why it wasn't just called "fourth" base. Then he talks about how the word home conjures up such warm images – no place like it. And in baseball, if you are lucky, you round first, and then if you are still lucky you round second, and if you can get past the scrappy shortstop, and you get really, really lucky, you can round third, and then he writes:

> And when it is given one to round third, a long journey seemingly over, the end in sight, then the hunger for home, the drive to rejoin one's earlier self and one's fellows, is a pressing, growing, screaming in the blood.

Heaven as home. The phrase dredges up a memory for me. It is fall revival time in Laurel Nazarene Church and Charles and Eleanor McKinney from Charleston, WV are the evangelists. Not only did he preach but they sang and one night they sang a song that became my Dad's favorite.

> If for the prize we have striven, after our labors are o'er,
> Rest to our souls will be given, on that eternal shore,
> Home of the soul,

Heaven was the home of the soul for my Dad. Every time I hear Anton Dvorak's "New World Symphony" I think of him. The theme – that was the only request my Dad had for his funeral – that theme – an old hymn – "Going Home." Two days before my Dad died he told Mama,

"Lucille, I heard singing last night. Sounded like Northeast Camp – tabernacle full – it was glorious."

Did my Dad really hear heaven's chorus? My head says, of course not, but my heart wonders.

Heaven as home. My Dad isn't the only one who thought that. How did Tennyson put it?

> Sunset and evening star – and one clear call for me,
> And may there be no moaning at the bar
> When I put out to sea.
> But such a tide as moving seems asleep,
> Too full for sound and foam,
> When that which drew from out the boundless deep
> Turns again home.

Heaven as home. Which suggests a caring God, and, in the end, a supportive creation. How else can you read these words from today's lesson?

> "They shall hunger no more, neither thirst anymore;
> The sun shall not strike them, nor any scorching heat.
> For the lamb in the midst of them will be their shepherd,
> And he will guide them to springs of living water;
> And God shall wipe away every tear from their eyes."

Heaven, to me, suggests a final stop – an eternal home.

Heaven – yes, I have my doubts. I still won't use the word a lot. But I will use it. Because I have moved from the questions I can't answer to the answers I can't escape. And heaven is one of those answers I can't escape.

Is it True

It has been ten years since I last spoke a word from a pulpit on Christmas Eve. I was beginning to feel like Zechariah of old, who was struck dumb, and thought, perhaps, that I would never ever get the chance to open my pulpit mouth at Christmas again.

Well, here I am, thanks to Mary and the Dumbarton Church worship committee. .

What faced me, after a decade of Advent and Christmas silence, was what on earth do I say? You get your shot – and if you have to wait ten more years – it could be your last shot. Do you suppose I can come up with something memorable to say, like Zechariah did?

> "And you, child, will be called the
>   prophet of the Most High;
> for you will go before the Lord
>   to prepare his ways. . . .
> to give light to those who sit in darkness
>   and in the shadow of death,
> to guide our feet into the way of peace."

And, frankly, the lessons I was assigned didn't help all that much. I tried – I really tried – to let them whisper something into my heart. The last time I remember dealing with the Luke passage was in the late seventies which, as I recall, childbirth was being looked upon as a social malady what with all the talk of a population explosion, and I used this text to talk about the blessings of bearing children. Do I need to tell you that not only have I never preached on the two other lessons I was given for this day: the Infancy Gospel of James and the Odes of Solomon; I didn't even know they existed. And during this all too typical – for me, at least – homiletical struggle, I had to put together our family Christmas letter, which was, in itself, a struggle.

You see, the euphoria of early November has all but dissipated itself with conditions in the world. I thought sure that the elections themselves would be a wake-up call. Then when the wise ones issued their sober-eyed findings on the Iraq war, I was sure that that would tip the balance toward sanity. But no, proving once more that denial is more than just a big river in Egypt.

I came home a couple Tuesdays ago from a breakfast group of retired liberal preachers. It's not that we are a closed group; it just seems that retired conservative preacher types don't seem to end up in the more progressive Lewes/Rehoboth, Delaware area. We did our usual Bush bashing over eggs and scrapple, and I was in no mood for working on our annual Christmas missive.

I noticed a Christmas book we pull out each year to plop down on the coffee table. It's a gorgeously bound volume carrying the title "Penhaligon's Scented Treasure of Christmas Verse and Prose." I had never cracked it.

On page 30 I came to an eight stanza poem titled, simply, "Christmas." I started to read

Well, that's nice, I thought, and only kept on reading because I do like poetry, and then came to stanza 6.

> "And is it true? And is it true,
>   this most tremendous tale of all,
>   That God was Man in Palestine
> And lives today in Bread and Wine."

Whoa, Nellie, as Keith Jackson used to say when he broadcast college football games. That's a mouthful.

The "and is it true" part of this poem triggered a memory of one of the few George Will columns I have saved. He opens with a quote from, as he puts it, "a sardonic British skeptic of the late 19th century" who said that etched in stone above all church doors should be this phrase: "Important, if true." And then Will ends the column with the sixth stanza of the poem I just cited.

I thought also of Frederick Buechner quoting Karl Barth who said that people come to church with a single question somewhere deep in their hearts: "Is it true?"

Is it – "this most tremendous tale of all?" One would gather that we certainly seem to think so. We pack the churches at this Holy Season. We sing, and seem to mean it, "Joy to the World, the Lord is come." We also sing, and seem to mean this, too, about a little town called Bethlehem that had its dark streets brightened by an everlasting light.

But is it true? It all depends, I think, on what you mean by true. Were there really shepherds abiding in the field as Luke says and Handel puts to such beautiful music? Did God really tell Joseph that he should take Mary, as his wife, because God had big plans for her? And what about that star that served as the Magi's GPS? True? It's possible, maybe. But we really don't know, for sure, do we?

And does it matter? For isn't there truth that goes deeper than the mere facts of history? Rudolph Bultmann thought so. He spoke of the gospels as myth. Myth – not as fairy tale – but myth as our attempt to put other-worldly truths in this-worldly language. Paul Tillich was saying somewhat the same thing when he wrote about God-talk as being meaningless talk. Paul was hanging around this same street corner when he said that faith, at its best, was hoping, simply because it was based on things that were unseen. The image he left us with was our trying to peek through a darkened glass. And it was he, wasn't it, who said, "Behold, I show you a mystery."

Not a bunch of unanswered questions that given enough time and enough smarts we can find out all the answers. Mystery, as an "authentic category of existence," is the way a writer from my long ago years put it.

No One Knows When It's a Good Day

Garrison Keillor says that we go to church to look at the mysteries, and "if you can't go to church, and, at least for a moment, be given transcendence, . . . then I can't see why anyone should go." Mark Trotter, who was, for years, pastor of The First United Methodist Church in San Diego put it this way:

> "Perhaps that is why the holiest night of the year is Christmas Eve, because it captures the mystery of his coming. The less said on Christmas Eve, the better. All that is needed is to tell the story, and then light some candles against the darkness, and sing 'Silent Night.'

"And is it true?" For me it is. True as in truth — at least the way I have defined it. A Methodist preacher, Harry Webb Farrington, who, in the early 1900's, served the same church in northern Maryland where my brother started out his ministerial life, wrote a hymn that never should have been scratched from the Methodist hymnal. The first verse goes:

> "I know not how that Bethlehem's Babe
> could in the God-head be,
> I only know the manger Child
> Has brought God's love to me."

And this is where I hang my Christmas hat. I'm somewhere close to the midwife in James' Infancy Gospel who cried, "How great this day is for me, for I have seen this new miracle." My faith doesn't demand an explanation or an answer for there are neither. My hope for the darkened streets that are a part of my world, the light that ever so dimly still shines, is based on my trust that in that Holy Land of long ago,

> "Love came down at Christmas,
>   Love, all lovely, Love Divine,
> Love was born at Christmas,
>   Star and angels gave the sign."

And if this world of ours is to be saved, it will be because enough of us allow that love that came down at Christmas to live in us.

> "Love shall be our token,
>   Love be yours and love be mine,
> Love to God and neighbor,
>   Love for plea and gift and sign."

Save the world by letting this Christmas star shine in our lives? The great ones have thought so. St. Augustine said: "Since you cannot do good to all, you are to pay special attention to those who, by accidents of time, or place, or circumstance, are brought into closer connection with you." And Mother Theresa did her one on one love dealing in the slums of Calcutta.

Last Sunday, Jack Abel, our pastor at Epworth told a story. Late one night he was coming out of the church and a man was lying on a bench that is in the little garden area out front. It was a chilly, but not cold, night. The man saw Jack look at him, and he asked if it would be alright for him to sleep there. Jack said that would be no problem, and started to walk away. Following Jack was a man who had been attending another meeting at the church. He went over to the man on the bench and asked him if he needed anything. The man said no. He tried again, "could you use a blanket." The man on the bench said, "Yes." "I have one in the car," the other man said. Jack stood watching all this. The other man went to his car and came back with – and at this point in the sermon Jack held up a gorgeous quilt – and tucked the man into his bench bed.

The next day, the man who had slept on the bench came into the church office with the quilt in hand. The spooky part is that when Jack checked with some of the people who had been present in the meeting in the church no one remembered seeing the man Jack described.

Is it really this simple? The one whose birth we celebrate thought so. The Good Samaritan. The woman at the well. Jairus' daughter. The woman who touched the hem of his garment. One touch at a time. One neighbor at a time.